Crocheted
Accessories

Crocheted Accessories

Vanessa Mooncie

THE GUILD OF MASTER CRAFTSMAN PUBLICATIONS

First published 2012 by
Guild of Master Craftsman Publications Ltd
Castle Place, 166 High Street, Lewes,
East Sussex BN7 1XU

ISBN 978-1-86108-829-1

A catalogue record for this book is available from
the British Library.

Publisher: Jonathan Bailey
Production Manager: Jim Bulley
Managing Editor: Gerrie Purcell
Senior Project Editor: Wendy McAngus
Editor: Nicola Hodgson
Managing Art Editor: Gilda Pacitti
Design: Rebecca Mothersole and Fineline Studios
Photography: Holly Joliffe and Anthony Bailey
Illustrations by Vanessa Mooncie

Set in Odstemplik and Kozuka Gothic Pro
Colour origination by GMC Reprographics
Printed and bound by 1010 Printing International Ltd in China

Contents

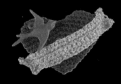

GALLERY

Fantail Dove
See page 49

Blackbird
See page 53

Bumblebee
See page 58

Sweetheart Tattoo
See page 67

Anchor Tattoo
See page 73

Loveheart Tattoo
See page 80

Battenberg
See page 88

Cherries
See page 93

Iced Doughnut
See page 99

Handful of Sweeties
See page 103

Wild Strawberry
See page 106

Giant Poppy
See page 115

Daffodil
See page 120

Pretty Posy
See page 127

Delicate Poppy
See page 135

Charms
See page 140

Heart Icon
See page 150

Oak Leaf & Acorn
See page 155

Triangle & Heart
See page 161

Mod Targets
See page 166

EQUIPMENT & MATERIALS

Equipment & Materials

The texture or colour of a yarn or thread can spark the start of an idea that, together with a small collection of simple and inexpensive tools, can be crocheted into a beautiful and unique accessory.

Equipment

Crocheting beautiful accessories requires only a few basic items of equipment. Hooks, of course, are the main requirement.

Crochet hooks

Originally, there were two ranges of hooks available in the UK – one for cotton and one for wool. A standard range for all thicknesses was then introduced in 1969. The old UK sizes are listed in the middle column of the chart overleaf. These sizes are not commonly used now, but might be handy to refer to if you are working from a vintage pattern or using vintage hooks. Metric hook sizes are listed on the left-hand side of the chart, while the US system of crochet hook sizing is given in the right-hand column. In this book we use metric hook sizes, but the UK and US equivalents are also given.

Crochet hooks traditionally come in aluminium and steel. They are also now commonly available in bamboo and in carved wood.

Hooks are available in a wide range of sizes: from 0.60mm (UK6:US14) to 1.75mm (UK2:US6) for use with fine threads; from 2.00mm (UK14:US-) to 11.50mm (UK-:USP/16) for thicker yarns; and enormous, outsized hooks for use with multiple strands of yarn.

Scissors

Small, sharp thread or embroidery scissors are best for trimming yarn ends, especially on delicate pieces.

Needles

Darning or tapestry needles are used to finish off the work in 4ply yarns. The rounded end prevents snagging. For projects using threads, a fine sewing needle with a sharp point is recommended. A thimble will come in handy, as it can be hard to get the needle through smaller pieces with compacted stuffing and closely woven stitches. Jewellery pliers are also a useful tool for this.

Pliers

There are three useful types of pliers:
• Round-nose pliers, for bending and looping the wire that decorates a finished piece of work.
• Side cutters, for cutting and trimming wires.
• Flat-nose pliers, for gripping wire and opening and closing wire rings. These are handy for use with both the round-nose and side-cutting pliers to hold fiddly wires while shaping and trimming them. They are also useful for pulling a needle through fine crocheted work.

Materials

Beautiful yarns and threads, along with materials for embellishments such as beads, will feed your imagination and inspiration for making inventive crochet pieces.

Yarns and threads

There is an abundance of beautiful yarns and threads available, and experimenting with different textures and materials can be very inspiring. An idea may evolve just by seeing how the fibre takes on a form while crocheting a simple swatch. Vintage threads that are faded or discoloured will give a unique finish. The same design crocheted once in mohair and again in a metallic yarn will have a completely different appearance and tactile quality, as would working both fibres together.

Materials do not have to be restricted to traditional wools, cottons and linens. String, strips of fabric, recycled carrier bags, ribbons and wire are just a few of the found objects that have the potential to create a work of art. Embroidery threads are lovely to work with, as they are available in many jewel colours and the strands can be separated to make finer pieces.

The tensions (or gauges) for the projects in this book are not important, and the sizes are given just as a guide. Trying projects using different hooks and materials will alter the proportions as well as the measurements. Working with fine thread and a larger hook will produce an open, lacy, loopy stitch, whereas a tighter, stiffer fabric will be constructed with a thicker yarn and finer hook.

Beads and findings

A piece of crochet can be enhanced by adding a little sparkle with a single faceted glass bead. Semi-precious gems, pearls, shells, metal, wood or acrylic beads will change the finished look of the crocheted accessory. Threading a bead onto a head pin to hang from a crocheted pendant provides an alternative to stitching the decoration and creates a more professional finish overall. From recycling a broken vintage necklace or attaching a single charm, the project can be transformed to create a personal piece or treasured gift.

Brooch bars come in varying sizes and in gold or silver colour, for use according to the dimensions of the work and the desired finish. Bars can be widely found in nickel-plated, silver-plated or gold-plated metal and in sterling silver, with drilled holes for stitching through, or without holes – these can be attached by sewing around the bar.

Toy stuffing

Polyester fibre toy stuffing is ideal for filling the crocheted pieces to give a solid, three-dimensional form.

PVA glue

PVA (polyvinyl acetate) glue is perfect for stiffening the crocheted work and keeping it in shape. It is water-soluble and can be diluted if required. PVA is washable, though if a finished crocheted accessory goes through the wash, it will need reshaping and a fresh coating of the glue applied to revitalize it.

Steel Crochet Hook Conversion

Metric (mm)	UK	US
0.60	6	14
-	5½	13
0.75	5	12
-	4½	11
1.00	4	10
-	3½	9
1.25	3	8
1.50	2½	7
1.75	2	6
-	1½	5

Aluminium Crochet Hook Conversion

Metric (mm)	UK	US
2.00	14	-
2.25	13	B/1
2.50	12	-
2.75	-	C/2
3.00	11	-
3.25	10	D/3
3.50	9	E/4
3.75	-	F/5
4.00	8	G/6
4.50	7	7
5.00	6	H/8
5.50	5	I/9
6.00	4	J/10
6.50	3	K/10½
7.00	2	-
8.00	0	L/11
9.00	00	M/13
10.00	000	N/15
11.50	-	P/16

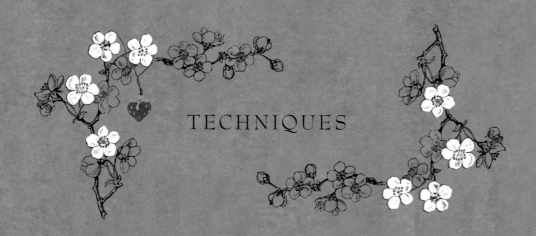

TECHNIQUES

Techniques

Crochet patterns are based on a few basic stitches. With just a hook and some yarn, starting with a simple slip loop, these stitches will provide endless possibilities for new designs and inspiration.

Slip knot

Take the end of the yarn and form it into a ring. Holding it in place between thumb and forefinger, insert the hook through the ring, catching the long end that is attached to the ball (see below left), and draw it back through. Keeping the yarn looped on the hook, pull through until the loop closes around the hook, ensuring it is not tight. Pulling on the short end of yarn will loosen the knot; pulling on the long end will tighten it.

Holding the hook

Hold the hook as you would a pencil, bringing your middle finger forward to rest near the tip of the hook (see below right). This helps control the movement of the hook, while the fingers of your other hand regulate the tension of the yarn. The hook should face you, pointing slightly downwards. The motion of the hook and yarn should be free and even, not tight. This will come with practice.

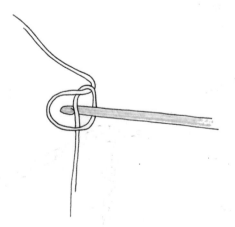

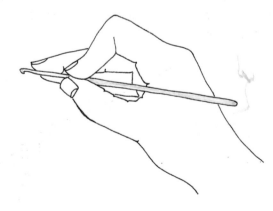

Holding the yarn

To hold your work and control the tension, pass the yarn over the first two fingers of your left hand (or right if you are left-handed), under the third finger, around the little finger and let the yarn fall loosely to the ball (see right). As you work, take the stitch you made between the thumb and forefinger of the same hand.

The hook is usually inserted through the top two loops of a stitch as you work, unless otherwise stated in a pattern. A different effect is produced when only the back loop of the stitch is picked up.

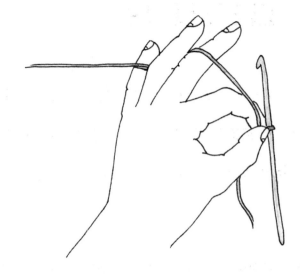

Chain (ch)

A length of chain stitches forms a foundation for crocheted fabrics. It can also be used as a decorative braid or a handle to finish a small purse or bag. It is a good idea to practise chain stitches until they are neat and even in size.

1 Pass the hook under and over the yarn that is held taut between the first and second fingers. This is called 'yarn round hook' (yrh). Draw the yarn through the loop on the hook. This makes one chain.

2 Repeat step 1 until you have as many chain stitches as required, keeping the thumb and forefinger of the left hand close to the hook.

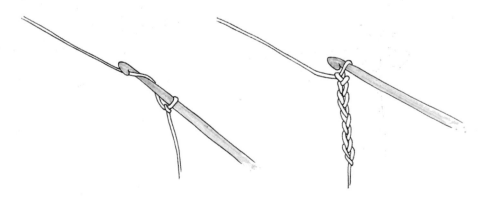

Slip stitch (sl st)

The slip stitch is used to join a round or as a narrow edging on a piece of crochet, often being worked into the back loop only of a stitch. This stitch is the smallest in height. No turning chains are needed to make slip stitches, unlike the double crochet (dc), which needs one chain, and the treble (tr), which needs three chains.

Make a practice chain of 10 stitches.

1 Insert hook into first stitch, yarn round hook, draw through both loops on hook. This forms 1 slip stitch.

Continue to end. This will give you 10 slip stitches (10 stitches).

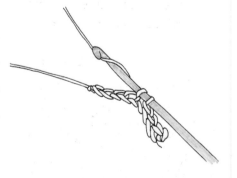

Double crochet (dc)

This stitch is deeper than the slip stitch. It is ideal for items that need a denser fabric, such as the Fantail Dove (see page 49) that require padding out with toy stuffing.

Make a practice chain of 17 stitches. Miss the first chain.

1 Insert hook from front into the next stitch, yarn round hook and draw back through the stitch (2 loops on hook).

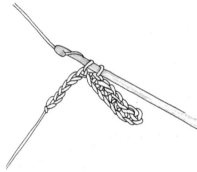

2 Yarn round hook, and draw through 2 loops (1 loop on hook). This makes one double crochet.

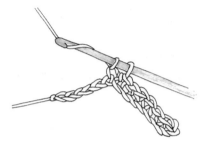

Repeat steps 1 and 2 to end.

On the foundation chain of 17 stitches you should have 16 double crochet stitches (16 stitches).

**DOUBLE CROCHET
(THROUGH BOTH LOOPS)**

Next row

Turn the work so the reverse side faces you. Make 1 chain. This is the turning chain, which helps keep a neat edge and does not count as a stitch. Repeat steps 1 and 2 to the end of the row. Continue until the desired number of rows is complete. Fasten off.

When working in double crochet, the hook is usually inserted under both loops of the stitch unless otherwise specified in a pattern. Working into just one loop of a stitch will produce a different effect.

**DOUBLE CROCHET
(THROUGH BACK LOOP ONLY)**

Half treble (htr)

The half treble is deeper than the double crochet stitch, creating a less firm fabric. The height of the stitch means that the work grows faster! This stitch is often used in between a double crochet and a treble stitch to form a smooth contour.

Make a practice chain of 17 stitches. Miss the first 2 chain (these count as the first half treble stitch).

1 Yarn round hook, insert hook into the next stitch, yarn round hook, draw back through stitch (3 loops on hook).

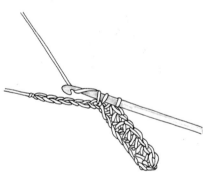

2 Yarn round hook, draw through all 3 loops (1 loop on hook). This forms 1 half treble.

Repeat steps 1 and 2 to the end of the row.
On the foundation chain of 17 stitches you should have 16 half treble stitches (16 stitches),

including the 2 chain at the beginning of the row, which was counted as the first stitch.

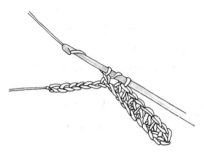

Next row

Turn the work so the reverse side faces you. Make 2 chain to count as the first half treble. Miss the first stitch of the previous row. Repeat steps 1 and 2 over the next 14 half treble of the last row, then work 1 half treble into the second of the 2 chain at the end of the row. Continue until the desired number of rows is complete. Fasten off.

HALF TREBLE

Treble (tr)

The treble stitch is longer than the previous stitches and forms quite an open fabric. The double treble and triple treble are variations of treble, made simply by winding the yarn round the hook once or twice more.

Make a practice chain of 18 stitches. Miss the first 3 chain (these count as the first treble stitch).

1 Yarn round hook, insert hook into the next stitch, yarn round hook, draw back through stitch (3 loops on hook).

2 Yarn round hook, draw through 2 loops (2 loops on hook).

3 Yarn round hook, draw through 2 loops (1 loop on hook). This forms 1 treble. Repeat steps 1–3 to row end.

On the foundation chain of 18 stitches you should have 16 trebles (16 stitches), including the 3 chain at the beginning of the row, counted as the first stitch.

Next row
Turn the work so that the reverse side faces you. Make 3 chain to count as the first treble. Miss the first stitch of the previous row. Repeat steps 1–3 to the end of the row, working 1 treble into the third of the 3 chain

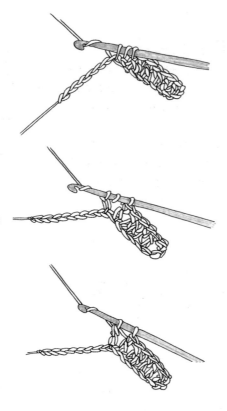

at the beginning of the last row. Continue until the desired number of rows is complete. Fasten off.

TREBLE

Double treble (dtr)

Make a practice chain of 19 stitches. Miss the first 4 chain (these count as the first double treble stitch).

1 Yarn round hook twice, insert hook into the next stitch, yarn round hook, draw back through stitch (4 loops on hook).

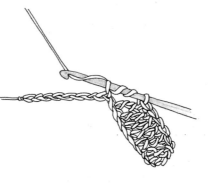

2 (Yarn round hook, draw through 2 loops) three times (1 loop on hook). This forms 1 double treble.

DOUBLE TREBLE

Triple treble (trtr)

Make a practice chain of 20 stitches. Miss the first 5 chain (these count as the first triple treble stitch).

1 Yarn round hook three times, insert hook into the next stitch, yarn round hook, draw back through stitch (5 loops on hook).

2 (Yarn round hook, draw through the 2 loops) four times (1 loop on hook). This forms 1 triple treble.

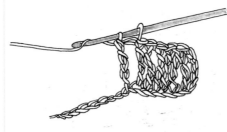

Repeat steps 1 and 2 to the end of the row.

On the foundation chain of 20 stitches you should have 16 double trebles (16 stitches), including the 5 chain at the beginning of the row, counted as the first stitch.

TRIPLE TREBLE

Repeat steps 1–2 to end of row.

On the foundation chain of 19 stitches you should have 16 trebles (16 stitches), including the 4 chain at the beginning of the row, counted as the first stitch.

Next row
Turn the work so the reverse side faces you. Make 4 chain to count as the first double treble. Miss the first stitch of the previous row. Repeat steps 1–2 to the end of the row. Continue until you have completed the desired number of rows. Fasten off.

Next row
Turn the work so the reverse side faces you. Make 5 chain to count as the first triple treble. Miss the first stitch of the previous row. Repeat steps 1 and 2 in each stitch to the end of the row. Continue until you have completed the required number of rows. Fasten off.

Joining in colours

When joining a new colour in the middle of a row, it is worked into the stitch preceding the one where the new shade is to start. The colour that is not in use is carried across the back of the work and hidden along the line of stitches being made using the contrast colour, keeping the crocheted fabric neat so either side of the finished work can be used.

Make a practice piece using two contrasting shades of yarn, A and B. Work a chain of 16 stitches in yarn A. Miss the first chain.

Row 1: Work 4 double crochet in A, insert hook in next stitch, yarn round hook, draw through stitch (2 loops on hook), yarn round hook with B, draw through both loops on hook, 4 double crochet in B, insert hook in next stitch, yarn round hook, draw back through stitch (2 loops on hook), yarn round hook with A, draw through both loops on hook, 5 double crochet in A, turn, 1 chain (does not count as a stitch) (15 stitches).

Rows 2–5: Repeat row 1, working the stitches over the strand of unused colours to cover.

Row 6: Working over the yarn not in use, work 4 double crochet in B, insert hook in next stitch, yarn round hook, draw through stitch (2 loops on hook), yarn round hook with A, draw through both loops on hook, 4 double crochet in A, insert hook in next stitch, yarn round hook, draw back through stitch (2 loops on hook), yarn round hook with B, draw through both loops on hook, 5 double crochet in B, turn, 1 chain (does not count as a stitch).

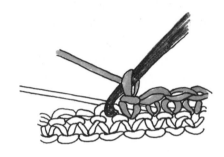

Rows 7–10: Repeat row 5.

Rows 11–15: Repeat row 1, missing the 1 chain at the end of the last row to complete the practice sample.

Fastening off

When you have finished your crochet piece, fasten off by cutting the yarn around 4¾in (12cm) from the work. Draw the loose end through the remaining loop, pulling it tightly.

Embroidery stitches

Some simple embroidery stitches may provide just the finishing touch you want to add to your crocheted accessory.

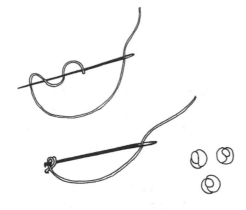

French knot

1 Bring the thread through to the right side of the work at the desired position where the French knot is to be made and hold it down with your left thumb. Wind the thread twice around the needle, still holding it firmly in place.

2 Insert the needle back into the work, close to the point where the thread first appeared. Pull the thread through to tighten the knot and bring the needle back through to the front of the work to start another French knot.

Bullion stitch

1 Using a needle with a narrow eye, work a back stitch by bringing the thread through to the front of the work at the position where the bullion stitch is to be made. Insert the needle just behind the point where the thread emerged and bring it out again to the required length of the finished bullion, keeping the needle in the fabric. Wind the thread around the needle as many times as required to cover the space.

2 Hold the coiled thread down and carefully pull the needle through. Turn the coiled thread back towards the point where the needle was inserted and pass the needle back into the same place, pulling the thread through to the back of the work until the stitch lies flat.

Project key

Now you are ready to make your accessories. These symbols will help you decide which ones to try.

Beginners

Intermediate

Advanced

BIRDS & BEES

Fantail Dove

These flighty fantailed doves form a confetti group of pretty brooches evocative of a magician's star turn, conjuring birds from his top hat that flit to the heights of the circus tent.

Materials

4ply yarn in any shade
Embroidery threads or oddments of
    yarn in black and yellow or
    metallic gold
2.50mm (UK12:US-) crochet hook
Small amount of toy stuffing
Darning needle
1in (2.5cm) brooch bar

Size

Actual measurements:
2in (5cm) from head to tail end
    (excluding fantail)

Tension

Not important

Method

The body is worked in continuous rounds of double crochet, starting from the base and finishing at the back. It is then folded and joined by slip stitching the last round of stitches together, leaving one end open for a few more rounds of double crochet to shape the head. The wings and tail are made separately and attached to the stuffed body. The dove is finished off with embroidered features and a brooch bar.

Body

Using 2.50mm hook and 4ply yarn, make 4 ch and join with a sl st to the first ch to form a ring.

Round 1: 1 ch (does not count as a st), into ring work 5 dc (5 sts).

Round 2 (inc): (Dc2inc) 5 times (10 sts).

Round 3: 1 dc in each st.

Round 4 (inc): (Dc2inc) 10 times (20 sts).

Round 5: 1 dc in each st.

Round 6 (inc): (Dc2inc, 1 dc) 10 times (30 sts).

Round 7: Fold piece and sl st together the outside loops of the next 10 sts on each side to join the back, 1 dc into each of the remaining 10 sts to form the start of the head.

Shape head

Rounds 8–9: 1 dc into each dc. Stuff the bird with toy stuffing, run gathering sts around the opening, draw up and fasten off. Work a row of running stitches before the start of the head shaping and gather up, but not too tightly, to indicate the neck.

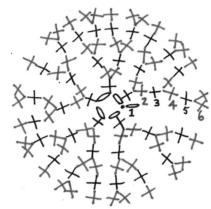

BODY ROUNDS 1–6

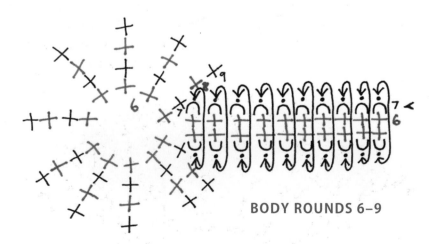

BODY ROUNDS 6–9

KEY	
⬭	chain (ch)
•	slip stitch (sl st)
+	double crochet (dc)
✕	dc2inc
T	half treble (htr)
ꝉ	treble (tr)
Ѵ	tr2inc
ꝭ	slip stitch together back loops on each side to join

Wing (make 2)

Using 2.50mm hook and 4ply yarn, make 11 ch.

Round 1: 1 dc into 2nd ch from hook, 1 htr in next ch, 1 tr in next 4 ch, 1 htr in next ch, 1 dc in next 2 ch, 2 dc in end ch.

Working down other side of ch, 1 dc in next 2 ch, 1 htr in next ch, 1 tr in next 4 ch, 1 htr in next ch, 1 dc in next ch (20 sts).

Round 2: 2 ch, 1 dc in each st to end, sl st into 2 ch sp. Fasten off, leaving long length at end.

WING

> ### Fancy that!
>
> Crochet is the sister craft to knitting and dates back as far as 1200BC, with specimens and examples found in Ancient Egypt. Reputedly, when the Israelites fled Egypt during the Exodus, they worked wool this way as they crossed the Sinai desert.

Fantail

Leaving a long length of yarn at the beginning, make 7 ch using 2.50mm hook and 4ply yarn.

Row 1 (RS): 1 dc into 2nd ch from hook, 1 dc into next 5 ch, turn (6 sts).

Row 2 (inc): 3 ch (counts as first tr), 1 tr in same st as 3 ch, (tr2inc) 5 times, turn (12 sts).

Row 3 (inc) (RS): 3 ch (counts as first tr), 1 tr in same st as 3 ch, (tr2inc) 11 times, turn (24 sts).

Row 4 (WS): 1 ch (does not count as a st), 1 dc in next 24 sts.

Fasten off and weave the long end of the yarn through the foundation chain at the narrow end of the fantail, gather up and stitch to the tail end of the body with the WS facing towards the head. The tail will curl naturally.

Making up

Join the wings to the sides of the body. Stitch from the neck to roughly halfway along the lower edge of each wing. Using oddments of black and gold or yellow embroider the eyes and beak. Sew a brooch bar to the base of the body.

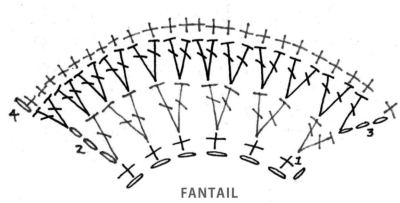

FANTAIL

Blackbird

The blackbird, with his golden beak and mellow song, is the inspiration for this elegant crocheted necklace, symbolizing the magical poise of this delicately sculpted bird.

Materials

Crochet thread 20 in black
Embroidery thread in blue-green
Oddments of thread in silver and
  yellow
0.75mm (UK5:US12) crochet hook
Tiny amount of toy stuffing
Sewing needle

Size

Actual measurements:
1¼in (3cm) from beak to tip of tail

Tension

Not important

Method

The blackbird body is like that of the Fantail Dove pattern (see pages 49–51), but uses a smaller hook and fine thread to create the tiny, delicate stitches. The wings and tail are made separately and attached to the body, along with a loop from which to hang the bird on the crocheted chain necklace. A loop at one end and a little bird egg button at the other fastens the chain.

Body

Using 0.75mm hook and black thread, make 4 ch and join with a sl st to the first ch to form a tiny ring.

Round 1: 1 ch (does not count as a st), into ring work 5 dc (5 sts).

Round 2 (inc): (Dc2inc) 5 times (10 sts).

Round 3: 1 dc in each dc.

Round 4 (inc): (Dc2inc) 10 times (20 sts).

Round 5: 1 dc in each st.

Round 6 (inc): (Dc2inc, 1 dc) 10 times (30 sts).

Round 7: Fold piece and sl st together the outside loops of the next 10 sts on each side to join the back, leaving the remaining 10 sts for the shaping of the head. Work 1 dc in each of the remaining 10 sts.

Shape head

Rounds 8–9: 1 dc into each dc. Stuff the bird with a tiny amount of toy stuffing, then run gathering sts around the head opening, draw up and secure with a few stitches. Work a row of running stitches before the start of the head shaping and draw up to indicate the neck.

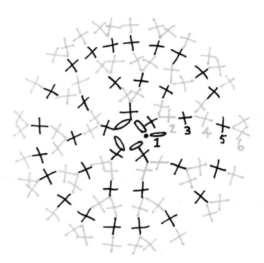

BODY ROUNDS 1–6

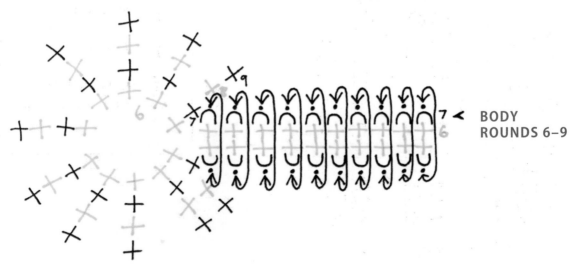

BODY ROUNDS 6–9

Wing (make 2)

With 0.75mm hook and black thread, make 8 ch.

Round 1: 1 dc into 2nd ch from hook, 1 dc in next 5 ch, 3 dc in end ch, 1 dc down other side of foundation chain to end (15 sts).

Round 2: 2 ch, 3 dc, 1 htr, 1 tr, 1 htr, 1 dc, sl st to next st, fasten off.

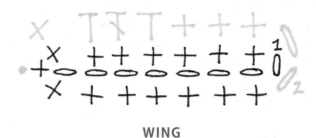

WING

Tail

Using 0.75mm hook and black thread, make 7 ch.

Row 1: 1 dc into 2nd ch from hook, 1 dc into next 5 ch, turn (6 sts).

Row 2: 1 ch (does not count as st), 3 dc, 3 htr, turn.

Row 3: 1 ch (does not count as st), 6 dc, turn.

Row 4: As row 3.

Row 5: 2 ch (does not count as st), 3 htr, 3 dc, turn.

Row 6: 1 ch (does not count as st), 6 dc, turn.

Row 7: Fold the piece lengthways and work 1 ch (does not count as st), (sl st tog the back loops of next 2 sts down edge of tail, 1 ch) 3 times. Fasten off.

KEY	
⬭	chain (ch)
•	slip stitch (sl st)
+	double crochet (dc)
X	dc2inc
T	half treble (htr)
⊤	treble (tr)
⏖	slip stitch together back loops on each side to join

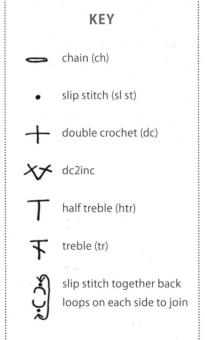

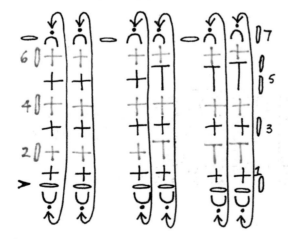

TAIL

Necklace

Egg

Using 0.75mm hook and 3 strands of green-blue embroidery thread together, make 4 ch and join with a sl st to first ch to form a ring.

Round 1: 1 ch (does not count as st), 6 dc into ring.

Round 2 (inc): (Dc2inc) 6 times (12 sts).

Rounds 3–6: 1 dc in each dc. Break thread, leaving a long length, stuff shape firmly and run a gathering st around the opening, draw up to close and fasten off.

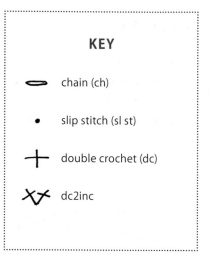

KEY

⬭ chain (ch)

• slip stitch (sl st)

✛ double crochet (dc)

✕ dc2inc

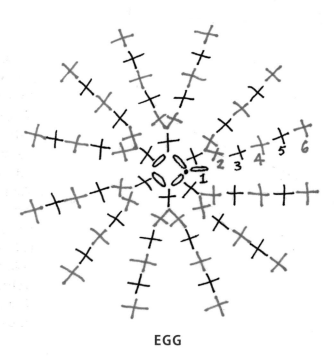

EGG

Loop and chain

Using 0.75mm hook and black crochet thread, make 16 ch and join with sl st to form a ring.

1 ch, 24 dc into ring, sl st to first dc.

Next: Work a chain measuring 16in (41cm), or to desired length. Fasten off, leaving a length of thread to stitch the finished chain securely to the gathered end of the egg. Weave in ends.

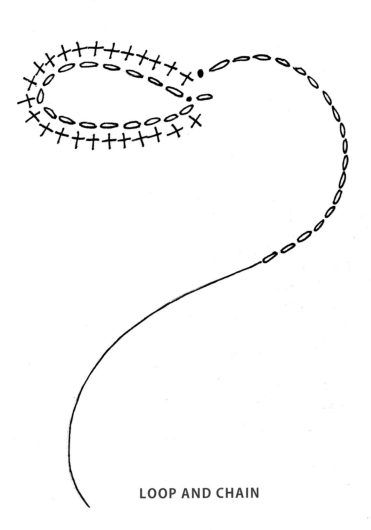

LOOP AND CHAIN

Making up

Sew the narrow end of the tail to the bird. Join the wings to the sides of the body. Using the oddments of silver and yellow, embroider the eyes and beak. Using 0.75mm hook and black thread, make 40 ch, join with a sl st to first ch to form a loop. Fasten off and stitch to the centre back of the bird. Weave in any loose ends. Attach the blackbird to the chain by looping the loop on the back of the bird over the chain of the necklace, and then thread the blackbird through the loop.

Bumblebee

This busy bumblebee is the perfect pin to dress any garment. The tiny, intricately worked wings give the appearance of delicate filigree.

Materials

Any crochet thread 20 in black (A) and yellow (B)
Embroidery thread in silver, using only 2 strands worked together (C)
0.75mm (UK5:US12) crochet hook
Tiny amount of toy stuffing
Sewing needle
PVA glue
Small paintbrush
Stickpin and stickpin protector

Size

Actual measurements:
⁵⁄₈in (1.5cm) in length with a wingspan of ⁷⁄₈in (2.25cm)

Tension

Not important

Method

The striped body is worked in continuous rounds with shaping to the abdomen and head. The pin is inserted through the back of the body from the inside before stuffing. The lower and upper wings are crocheted in one piece for each side and attached to the finished body after stiffening them with thin layers of PVA glue.

Body

Using 0.75mm hook and A, make
4 ch and join with sl st to first ch to
form a ring.

Round 1: 1 ch (does not count as
st), 6 dc into ring (6 sts).

Round 2 (inc): Join in B, (dc2inc) 6
times (12 sts).

Round 3 (inc): With A, (dc2inc, 2 dc)
4 times (16 sts).

Round 4: With B, 1 dc in each st.

Round 5 (dec): With A, (dc2dec, 2
dc) 4 times (12 sts).

Round 6: As round 4.

Shape head

Round 7 (dec): With A, (dc2dec,
4 dc) twice (10 sts).

Rounds 8–9: With A, 1 dc in each st.
Fasten off, leaving a long length
of thread.

Slip the pin through the centre back
of the bee from the inside, so it
appears between rounds 4 and 5 on
the outside of the work. It may need
a bit of jiggling to get it in place. Put
the protector onto the end of the
pin before continuing. Holding the
top of the pin so the pad sits flat
against the inside, stuff the body
firmly, pushing the stuffing in with
the wrong end of the crochet hook.
Work a running stitch around the
opening at the head, draw up to
close and fasten off.

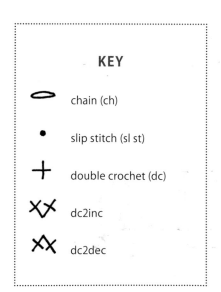

KEY

◯   chain (ch)

•   slip stitch (sl st)

✛   double crochet (dc)

✕✕   dc2inc

ㅅㅅ   dc2dec

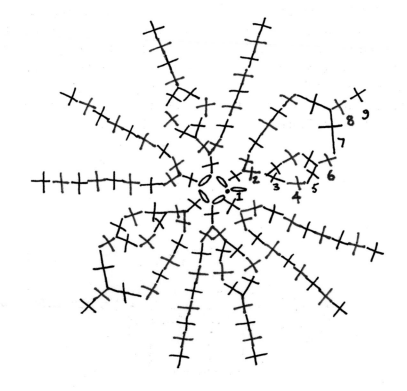

BODY

Double wing (make 2)

Upper wing

Using C and 0.75mm hook, make 6 ch.

Round 1: 1 dc into 2nd ch from hook, 1 dc in next 3 ch, 3 dc in end ch, 1 dc down other side of foundation ch to end (11 sts).

Round 2: 2 ch, 1 dc, 1 htr, 1 tr, 1 htr, 3 dc, 1 htr, 1 tr, 1 htr, 1 dc, sl st to 2 ch sp. Do not fasten off.

Lower wing

Make 8 ch.

Round 1: 1 dc into 2nd ch from hook, 1 dc in next 3 ch, 3 dc in next ch, miss out last 2 ch, work 1 dc in each ch down opposite side of foundation ch (11 sts).

Round 2: 2 ch, 1 dc, 1 htr, 1 tr, 1 htr, 1 dc, sl st to next st. Fasten off,

leaving a long length and weave in shorter end.

Pull into shape and paint the backs of the wings carefully with a little PVA glue. Leave to dry completely.

Making up

Position the lower wing so it sits at an angle below the larger upper wing and, using the long length of thread left, secure with a couple of stitches before attaching the wings to the side of the bee. Repeat for the second set of wings to mirror the first and stitch to the other side. Paint another coat of glue on the underside of the wings and leave again to dry completely.

KEY	
⬯	chain (ch)
•	slip stitch (sl st)
+	double crochet (dc)
T	half treble (htr)
⊤̄	treble (tr)

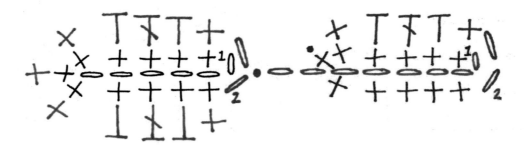

UPPER WING   **LOWER WING**

Variation

Necklace

This bee looks lovely as a pendant hanging by a link from a necklace. Make the bee, as above, omitting the stickpin. For the link, make 10 ch using 0.75mm hook and A, join with a sl st to first ch to form a ring. Into the ring work 14 dc, sl st to first dc and fasten off, leaving a long length of thread. Sew the link to the underside of the bee so the top of it sits hidden behind the head. Leave a gap at the top of the link to thread the chain through.

Button

Using 0.75mm hook and A, make 4 ch and join with sl st to first ch to form a ring.

Round 1: 1 ch (does not count as st), 6 dc into ring (6 sts).

Round 2 (inc): (Dc2inc) 6 times (12 sts).

Rounds 3–5: 1 dc in each dc. Fasten off, leaving long length, thread through sts, stuff firmly, gather up and fasten off.

KEY

⬭	chain (ch)
•	slip stitch (sl st)
+	double crochet (dc)
✕✕	dc2inc

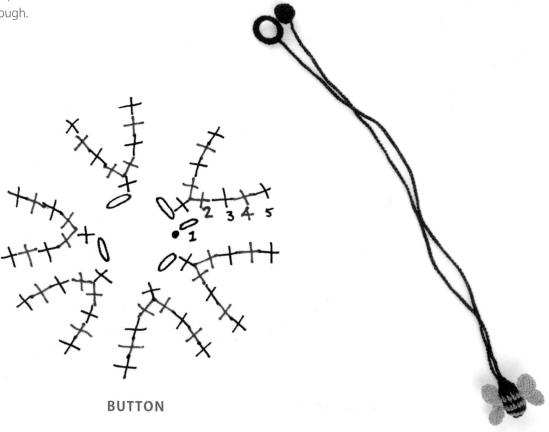

BUTTON

Chain and loop

Using 0.75mm hook and A, make 16 ch and join with sl st to first ch to form a ring.

1 ch, 24 dc into ring, sl st to first dc.

Next: Work a chain measuring 17in (43cm), or to desired length, allowing an extra ⅝in (1.5cm) for attaching the bee. Fasten off and sew button to end. Fold the chain in the middle to form a loop and thread it through the link, using a crochet hook to catch it and draw it through. Pass the ends of the necklace through the looped chain. Pull tightly on ends to secure.

Fancy that!

The beautiful bumblebee is associated in art with the Golden Age when humankind lived harmoniously with nature, feeding on berries, acorns and honey. Cupid is often depicted stealing a honeycomb and suffering a bee sting.

Variation: Threads

The look of the finished bee can be transformed simply by changing the threads. Experiment with a fine cotton or linen for the wings. Gold-coloured machine embroidery thread can be used together with the yellow for the stripes, which will catch the light for extra sparkle.

CHAIN AND LOOP

Sweetheart Tattoo

A blend of stitches, colour and texture form the symbols of the rose and the heart in a celebration of love. Here the two combine to create a traditional-style tattoo brooch.

Materials

Small amount of 4ply yarn in red (A), oddments of 4ply yarn in cream (B), pale yellow (C), bright blue (D), dark blue (E), pale pink (F), bright pink (G) and metallic black (H)
2.50mm (UK12:US-) crochet hook
Small amount of toy stuffing
Darning needle
1¼in (3cm) brooch bar

Size

Actual measurements:
Widest part measures 2¾in (7cm) excluding flowers
Longest part measures 2⅛in (5.5cm)

Tension

Not important

Method

The heart is crocheted in continuous rounds. The ribbon is worked in rows, decreasing then increasing the stitches at each end to form the shaping. The roses are formed from a length of crocheted scalloped petals, which, when wound into a spiral, creates the finished bloom.

Heart

Using 2.50mm hook and A, wind yarn round finger a couple of times to form a ring. Insert hook into ring, catch yarn and draw through, 1 ch (does not count as st).

Round 1: Into ring work 6 dc (6 sts).

Round 2: 1 dc in each dc. Pull on short end of yarn to close ring.

Round 3 (inc): (Dc2inc) 6 times (12 sts).

Round 4: 1 dc in each dc.

Round 5 (inc): (Dc2inc) 12 times (24 sts).

Rounds 6–7: 1 dc in each dc.

Round 8 (inc): (Dc2inc, 1 dc) 12 times (36 sts).

Rounds 9–10: 1 dc in each dc.

Shape top

**Round 11: 1 dc in each of next 9 dc, turn, 1 dc in opposite 9 dc to form beginning of top shaping (18 sts).

Rounds 12–14: 1 dc in each of the 18 dc.

Fasten off, leaving long length of yarn. Rejoin yarn to remaining 18 sts and work 4 rounds of dc in each st to match the first side. Stuff the heart firmly, thread long end of yarn through the stitches of last round of top shaping, gather up and fasten off neatly. Repeat on other side of shaping. Weave in ends.**

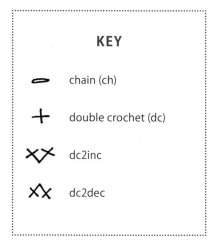

KEY

⬭	chain (ch)
+	double crochet (dc)
⤬⤬	dc2inc
⤫⤫	dc2dec

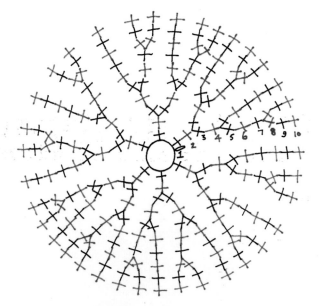

HEART ROUNDS 1–10

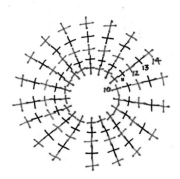

HEART TOP-SHAPING ROUNDS 10–14

Ribbon

Using 2.50mm hook and H, make 38 ch.

Row 1 (dec): 1 dc into 3rd ch from hook, 1 dc in each of next 33 ch, dc2dec, turn (35 sts).

Row 2 (dec): Miss first dc, 1 dc into each of next 32 dc, dc2dec, turn (33 sts).

Row 3 (inc): 3 ch, 1 dc in 2nd and 3rd ch from hook, 1 dc into next 33 dc, turn (35 sts).

Row 4 (inc): 3 ch, 1 dc into 2nd and 3rd ch from hook, 1 dc into next 34 sts, sl st into next st.
Fasten off.

RIBBON

Rose (make 3)

Using 2.50mm hook and B, make 8 ch.

Row 1: 1 dc into 2nd ch from hook, (4 ch, 1 dc in next ch) 6 times, turn.

Row 2: *((1 dc, 8 tr, 1 dc) in next 4 ch sp)* 4 times. Join in C and work from * to * twice. Fasten off, leaving long length of yarn. Weave in short ends, then with WS of work on the inside, wind the petals into a tight spiral and secure with a few stitches. Make a rose using D with E and another using F with G, in place of B and C.

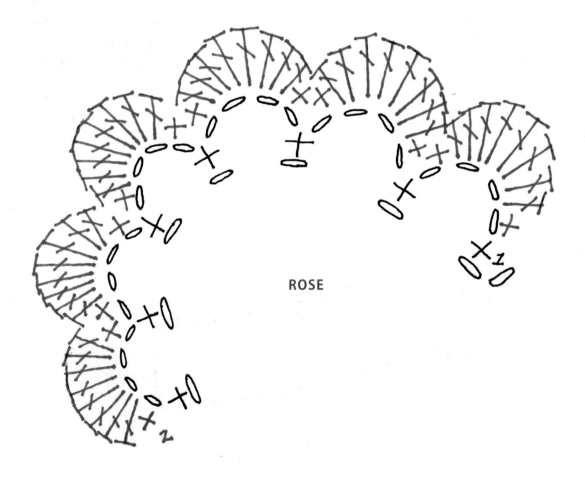

ROSE

Making up

The ribbon can be embroidered with a name or word, if so desired, such as 'sweet', 'true' or 'love', using embroidery threads or seed beads before being attached to the finished heart. Position the ribbon over the heart at a slight angle, from the left going down to the right, wrapping it around the sides to the back and folding both ends towards the front again to give the draped effect. Stitch in place (see illustration below). Sew the roses to the left side and attach a brooch bar to the back, placing it just below the top shaping. Paint a thin layer of PVA glue on the backs of the shaped ends of the ribbon to keep them in shape. Leave to dry completely before wearing.

Variation

Make a simple version of the sweetheart tattoo brooch by following rows 1 to 9 of the pattern as given for the heart. Miss out row 10 and continue from ** to **. Make the ribbon, as before, and attach it across the finished, smaller heart in the same way. Attach a brooch bar to the back, just below the top shaping.

Fancy that!

The rose is an enduring symbol of devotion, often linked to the goddess of love, Venus, by Renaissance writers and artists, because of its fragrance and beauty. A rose entwining a heart symbolizes true romance, the flower representing the sweetheart of the wearer.

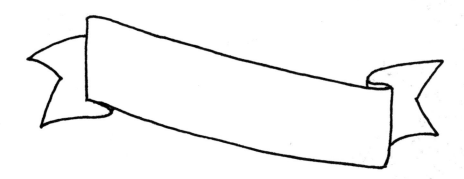

Anchor Tattoo

Ahoy there sailor! A rich blend of the jovial and sincere imbue this brooch design. It brings together stability and protection, symbolized by the anchor, with all the fun of the seaside!

Materials

Small amount of 4ply yarn in dark blue (A), oddments of 4ply in pale blue (B) (use DOUBLED) and metallic black (C)
2.00mm (UK14:US-) and 2.50mm (UK12:US-) crochet hooks
Small amount of toy stuffing
Darning needle
1¼in (3cm) brooch bar

Size

Actual measurements:
Widest part measures 3in (7.5cm)
Longest part measures 3⅜in (8.5cm)

Tension

Not important

Method

Each piece of the anchor is made separately. The main parts are stuffed before stitching the pieces together. A simple length of crocheted chain is draped around the anchor, and a ribbon, worked in rows with the shaping formed by decreasing and increasing the stitches, is added to the front. A brooch bar attached to the back finishes the anchor.

Anchor shank

Starting at the base, using 2.00mm hook and A, make 4 ch and join with a sl st to first ch to form a ring, 1 ch (does not count as a st).

Round 1: Into ring work 5 dc (5 sts).

Round 2: (Dc2inc) 5 times (10 sts).

Rounds 3–6: 1 dc into each dc.

Round 7 (dec): (Dc2dec, 3 dc) twice (8 sts).

Rounds 8–16: 1 dc in each dc. Fasten off, leaving long length of yarn.

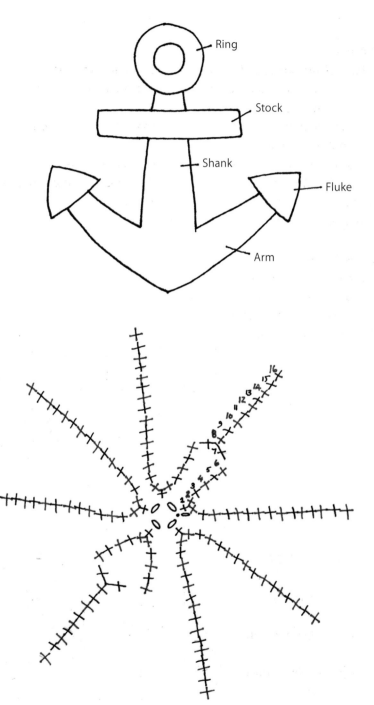

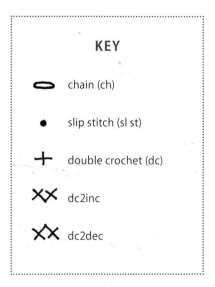

KEY

⬭ chain (ch)

● slip stitch (sl st)

✛ double crochet (dc)

✕✕ dc2inc

✕✕ dc2dec

ANCHOR SHANK

Stock

Using 2.00mm hook and A, wind yarn round finger a couple of times to form a ring. Insert hook into ring, catch yarn and draw through, 1 ch (does not count as st).
Round 1: Into ring work 8 dc (8 sts).
Rounds 2–5: 1 dc in each dc.
Pull tightly on short end of yarn to close ring.

Divide for openings

The following is worked in rows:
Row 6: 1 dc in next 3 dc, turn (3 sts).
Rows 7–9: 1 ch (does not count as a st), 1 dc in next 3 dc, turn.
Fasten off.

Complete other side

Rejoin yarn to remaining 5 sts on round 6.
Next: Sl st into first dc, rep rows 6–9.

Join the two sides

The following is continued in rounds:

Round 10: With RS facing, 1 ch (does not count as a st), *1 dc in next 3 dc, 1 ch*, continuing onto the other side of work to join, rep from * to *, sl st to first dc (8 sts).
Round 11: (1 dc in next 3 dc, 1 dc in next ch) twice.
Rounds 12–14: 1 dc in each dc.
Fasten off.

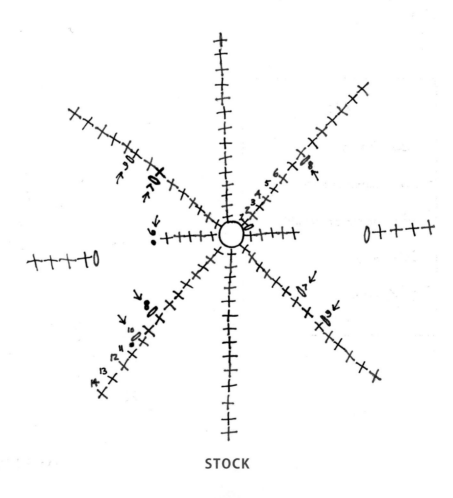

STOCK

KEY

⊙ chain (ch)

• slip stitch (sl st)

+ double crochet (dc)

Ring (make 2)

Using 2.50mm hook and A, make
8 ch and join with sl st to first ch to
form a ring.
Next: 1 ch (does not count as a st),
24 dc into ring. Fasten off.
Make another ring to match the
first, do not fasten off.

Join rings

With WS tog, sl st into back loop
of next 20 sts on both pieces to join.
Fasten off, leaving long length
of yarn.

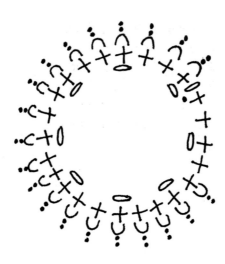

RING (MAKE 2)

KEY	
⬭	chain (ch)
•	slip stitch (sl st)
+	double crochet (dc)
⁝⌒	slip stitch into back loop of stitches on both pieces to join

Arm

Using 2.00mm hook and A, make
19 ch.
Row 1: 1 dc into 2nd ch from hook,
1 dc into next 17 ch, turn (18 sts).
Row 2: 1 ch (does not count as a st),
1 dc in each of next 8 dc, (dc2inc)
twice, 1 dc in each of remaining 8
dc, turn (20 sts).
Row 3: 1 ch (does not count as a st),
1 dc in each of next 9 dc, (dc2inc)
twice, 1 dc in each of next 9 dc, turn
(22 sts).

Row 4: 1 ch (does not count as a st),
1 dc in each of next 9 dc, (dc2dec)
twice, 1 dc in each of next 9 dc, turn
(20 sts).
Row 5: 1 ch (does not count as a st),
1 dc in each of next 8 dc, (dc2dec)
twice, 1 dc in each of remaining 8
dc, turn (18 sts).
Row 6: 1 dc in each dc. Fasten off.

KEY	
⬭	chain (ch)
+	double crochet (dc)
✕✕	dc2inc
✕✕	dc2dec

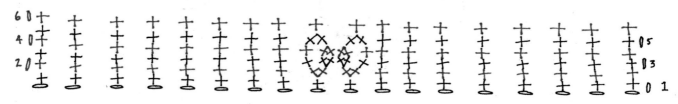

ARM

Fluke *(make 2)*

Using 2.00mm hook and A, wind yarn round finger a couple of times to form a ring. Insert hook into ring, catch yarn and draw through, 1 ch (does not count as st).

Round 1: Into ring work 6 dc (6 sts).

Round 2: 1 dc into back loop of each dc.

Round 3: (Dc2inc, 1 dc) into back loops, 3 times (9 sts).

Round 4: (Dc2inc, 2 dc) into back loops, 3 times (12 sts).

Round 5: (Dc2inc, 2 dc) into back loops, 4 times (16 sts). Pull tightly on short end to close ring. Fasten off, leaving a long length of yarn.

KEY	
⬭	chain (ch)
+	double crochet (dc)
⊥C	dc into back loop
⨉C	dc2inc into back loop

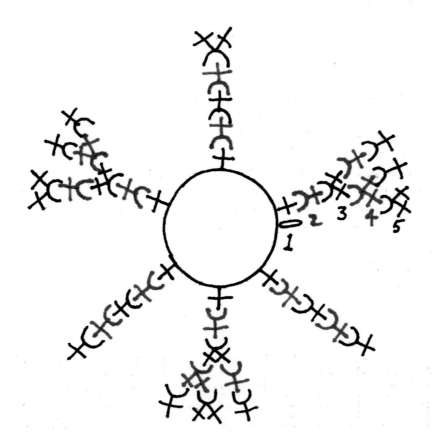

FLUKE (MAKE 2)

Chain

Using 2.50mm hook and B DOUBLED, make 35 ch. Fasten off, leaving a long length of yarn.

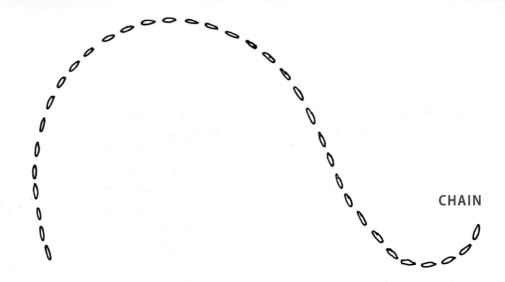

CHAIN

Ribbon

Using 2.00mm hook and C, make 32 ch.

Row 1 (dec): 1 dc into 3rd ch from hook, 1 dc in each of next 27 ch, dc2dec, turn (29 sts).

Row 2 (dec): Miss first dc, 1 dc into each of next 26 dc, dc2dec, turn (27 sts).

Row 3 (inc): 3 ch, 1 dc in 2nd and 3rd ch from hook, 1 dc into next 27 dc, turn (29 sts).

Row 4 (inc): 3 ch, 1 dc into 2nd and 3rd ch from hook, 1 dc into next 28 sts, sl st into next st. Fasten off.

A loved one's name, or a word such as 'true' or 'hope', can be added to the ribbon in embroidery or beading, or simply left blank, as desired.

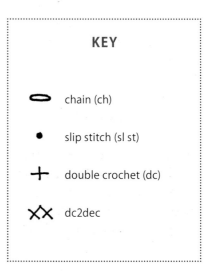

KEY

⬭ chain (ch)

• slip stitch (sl st)

+ double crochet (dc)

ХХ dc2dec

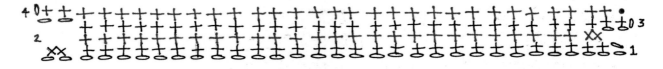

RIBBON

Making up

Stuff the shank using the wrong end of the crochet hook to push the stuffing right to the base of the work. Use the fastened-off long length of yarn to gather the top and fasten off. Stuff the first half of the stock, finishing at the opening in the middle. Use the end of the hook to push the stuffing right in. Slip the divided middle of the piece over the narrow end of the shank and stitch in position ½in (1.25cm) from the top (see photograph below). Stuff the open end of the stock, gather the end and fasten off.

Place the open end of the ring over the narrow top of the shank, and stitch in place. Fold the arm of the anchor and slip the wide end of the shank into the shaped centre of the arm. Stitch in place and then join the seams on each side. Stuff each side of the arm, teasing it back into shape as you go. Run a gathering stitch around each end and draw up to close. Slip a fluke over one end of the arm so there is a gap on each side. Sew the overlapping edges together and slip stitch the fluke in place on the arm. Repeat on other side.

Attach the chain using the long length of yarn, draping it around the anchor and fixing in place with a few stitches. Fold the shaped edge on the right of the ribbon to the back then fold again to the front of the work so it sits above the upper edge. Repeat for the left side so it sits below the lower edge. Stitch folded edges in position (see the illustration below) and attach across the front of the anchor.

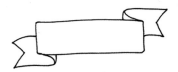

Weave in ends. Sew brooch bar across the back of the stock (see photograph below, right).

Variation

Make the anchor in the same way, omitting the ribbon, for an alternative look.

Fancy that!

Crochet did not become popular until the early 1800s. It was previously classified as 'nuns' work', referring to a time when woollen crafts were almost entirely an ecclesiastical art, requiring high standards of technique and beauty.

Loveheart Tattoo

This necklace captures the symbolism of love and protection within the tattoo tradition, elegantly presenting it as a treasured keepsake with the adornment of a simple charm.

Materials

Any crochet thread 20 in red (A)
   and black (C)
Embroidery thread in silver, using
   only 2 strands worked together (B)
0.75mm (UK5:US12) crochet hook
Small amount of toy stuffing
Sewing needle
Swallow charm

Size

Actual measurements:
Widest part measures 1¼in (3cm)
Longest part measures ⅞in
   (2.25cm)

Tension

Not important

Method

The heart and ribbon are made in a similar way to the Sweetheart Tattoo (see pages 67–71). However, by using a smaller hook and thread, rather than 4ply yarn, this finished piece is more delicate and fine-looking. The heart is decorated with a swallow charm, stitched in place at the end, before attaching the pendant to the crocheted chain.

Heart

Using 0.75mm hook and A, make 4 ch and join with a sl st to the first ch to form a tiny ring.

Round 1: 1 ch (does not count as a st), into ring work 5 dc (5 sts).

Round 2 (inc): (Dc2inc) 5 times (10 sts).

Round 3: 1 dc in each dc.

Round 4 (inc): (Dc2inc) 10 times (20 sts).

Rounds 5–6: 1 dc in each dc.

Round 7 (inc): (Dc2inc, 1 dc) 10 times (30 sts).

Round 8: 1 dc in each dc.

Round 9 (inc): (Dc2inc, 2 dc) 10 times (40 sts).

Rounds 10–11: 1 dc in each dc.

KEY

⬭   chain (ch)

•   slip stitch (sl st)

✛   double crochet (dc)

✕   dc2inc

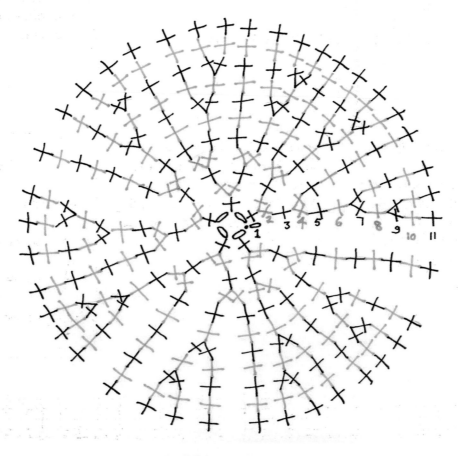

HEART ROUNDS 1–11

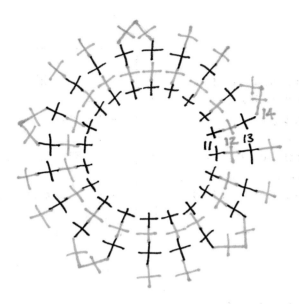

HEART TOP-SHAPING ROUNDS 11–14

Shape top

Round 12: *1 dc in next 10 dc, turn, 1 dc in opposite 10 dc to form first side of top shaping (20 sts).

Round 13: 1 dc in each of 20 dc.

Round 14 (dec): (Dc2dec, 2 dc) 5 times (15 sts).

Break thread, leaving long length.*

Rejoin A to other side and rep from * to * to match first side.

Stuff the heart firmly, then gather each side of the top shaping and fasten off neatly.

Ribbon

Using 0.75mm hook and B, make 30 ch.

Row 1 (dec): 1 dc into 3rd ch from hook, 1 dc in each of next 25 ch, dc2dec, turn (27 sts).

Row 2 (dec): Miss first dc, 1 dc into each of next 24 dc, dc2dec, turn (25 sts).

Row 3 (inc): 3 ch, 1 dc in 2nd and 3rd ch from hook, 1 dc into next 25 dc, turn (27 sts).

Row 4 (inc): 3 ch, 1 dc into 2nd and 3rd ch from hook, 1 dc into next 26 sts, sl st into next st.

Fasten off.

KEY

⬭	chain (ch)
•	slip stitch (sl st)
+	double crochet (dc)
✗✗	dc2dec

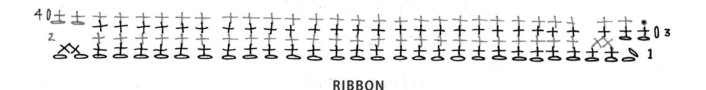

RIBBON

Necklace

Link

Using 0.75mm hook and A, make 10 ch, join with a sl st to first ch to form a ring. Into the ring work 14 dc, sl st to first dc and fasten off, leaving a long length of thread.

Button

Using 0.75mm hook and C, make 4 ch and join with sl st to first ch to form a ring.

Round 1: 1 ch (does not count as st), 6 dc into ring (6 sts).

Round 2 (inc): (Dc2inc) 6 times (12 sts).

Rounds 3–5: 1 dc in each dc. Fasten off leaving long length, thread through sts, stuff firmly, gather up and fasten off.

Chain and loop

Using 0.75mm hook and C, make 16 ch and join with sl st to first ch to form a ring.

1 ch, 24 dc into ring, sl st to first dc.

Next: Work a chain measuring 17in (43cm), or to desired length, allowing an extra ⅝in (1.5cm) for attaching the heart. Fasten off and sew button to end.

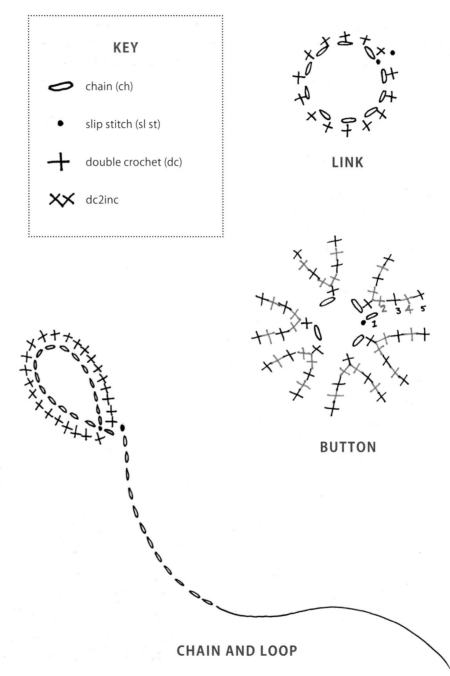

KEY

⬭ chain (ch)

• slip stitch (sl st)

+ double crochet (dc)

✕✕ dc2inc

LINK

BUTTON

CHAIN AND LOOP

Making up

Position the ribbon at an angle across the heart. Sew in place. The stiff nature of the metallic thread means that it keeps its shape quite well, though the ends can be painted with a little PVA glue to stiffen them, if desired. Stitch the swallow charm to the top shaping at the front, above the lower end of the ribbon. Make the stitch that holds the swallow a little loose to allow the bird to move. Attach the link just below the top shaping at the back, laying it flat against the heart and leaving a gap at the top of the link to thread the chain through. Fold the chain in the middle to form a loop and thread it through the link, using a crochet hook to catch it and draw it through for about 1in (2.5cm). Pass the ends of the chain through the loop. Pull tightly on the ends to close the loop and secure.

Variation: Brooch

Make the Love Heart Tattoo in the same way, leaving out the link and necklace. Stitch a small brooch bar to the widest part, just below the shaping, at the back of the piece.

Fancy that!

Considered a luxury, in the 19th century crochet was taught to the young ladies of the upper classes, who created intricate items to decorate their clothing and homes. The lower classes would be encouraged to make do and mend, knitting basic necessities.

SWEETS & TREATS

Battenberg

The quirky cake is brought to life through the combination of pastel yarns and symmetry of design, creating a dainty brooch to adorn a garment or double up as a pincushion!

Materials

Oddments of 4ply yarn in yellow (A)
    and pink (B)
Small amount of DK yarn in
    yellow (C)
2.50mm (UK12:US-) crochet hook
Toy stuffing
Darning needle
1¼in (3cm) brooch bar

Size

Actual measurements:
2³⁄₈in (6cm) wide x 2³⁄₈in (6cm) long
⁷⁄₈in (2.25cm) deep

Tension

Not important

Pattern notes

Ensure the unused yarns are held at the back of the work when crocheting the front of the Battenberg slice.

When starting row 7, keep the yarn that is drawn across the back loose, so as not to pucker the work. The strands can be crocheted over when working rows 7 and 8.

Method

The front of the cake is made as a square patch, worked in rows, joining in the pink yarn to create the traditional Battenberg sponge. The yellow back is also worked in rows as a patch to match the size of the front, and then continued in rounds to form the marzipan sides.

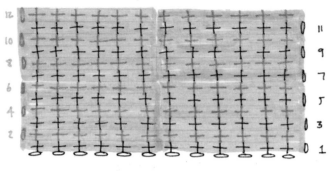

FRONT

Front

Using 2.50mm hook and A, make 13 ch.

Row 1 (RS): 1 dc into 2nd ch from hook, 1 dc in each of next 4 ch, insert hook in next ch, yrh, draw through loop, catch yarn B with hook, draw through both loops on hook, 1 dc in each of next 6 dc in B, turn (12 sts).

Row 2 (WS): In B, 1 ch (does not count as a st), 1 dc in each of next 5 dc, insert hook in next ch, yrh, draw through loop, catch yarn A with hook, draw through both loops on hook, 1 dc in each of next 6 dc in A, turn.

Row 3: In A, 1 ch (does not count as a st), 1 dc in each of next 5 dc, insert hook in next ch, yrh, draw through loop, catch yarn B with hook, draw through both loops on hook, 1 dc in each of next 6 dc in B, turn.

Rows 4 & 6: As row 2.

Row 5: As row 3.

Row 7: As row 2.

Row 8: As row 3.

Rows 9–12: Rep rows 7–8 twice. Fasten off.

Back and sides

Using 2.50mm hook and C, make 13 ch.

Row 1: 1 dc into 2nd ch from hook, 1 dc in each of next 11 ch, turn (12 sts).

Row 2: 1 ch (does not count as a st), 1 dc in each dc to end, turn.

Rows 3–12: As row 2.

Marzipan edges

The following is worked in rounds:

Round 13: 1 ch (does not count as a st), (dc2inc, 1 dc in each of next 10 sts) 4 times, working into each dc of row 12, evenly down the sts at the edge of each row and into each of the foundation ch (48 sts).

Rounds 14–15: 1 dc in each dc, turn. Do not fasten off.

Making up

With WS tog and RS of front piece facing, work 1 dc through each st, and, at the same time, through each stitch of marzipan to join, working 2 dc at each corner of the marzipan edge, with 1 ch in between, into the 1 dc at each corner of the front. Leave a gap to push the stuffing into, filling the cake firmly, before closing, shaping the slice by pinching the corners and pulling on the straight edges. Sl st to first dc and fasten off. Weave in the ends. Sew the brooch bar across the back so it sits a third of the way down from the top.

Fancy that!

The Battenberg cake is said to have been created to celebrate the marriage of Queen Victoria's granddaughter, Princess Victoria of Hesse, to Prince Louis of Battenberg in 1884. The four sponge sections inside the marzipan represent the four Battenberg princes.

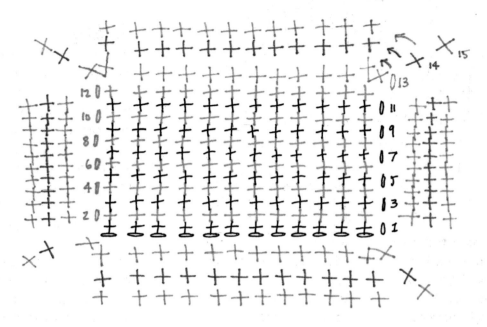

BACK AND MARZIPAN EDGES

Round 15 of
Marzipan Edges

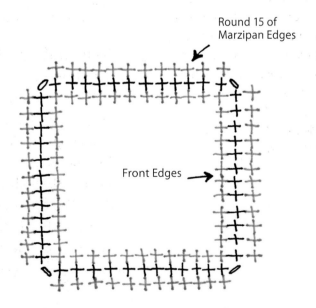

Front Edges

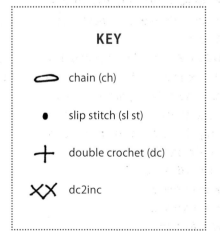

KEY

⬭ chain (ch)

● slip stitch (sl st)

+ double crochet (dc)

XX dc2inc

Stitches worked into both Front Edges and Marzipan Edges to join

Cherries

Full of the vibrancy of summer, the vintage fashion cherry icon is here used to stylish effect as a delicious brooch, blending simple stitches to form a delight on any lapel.

Materials
Oddments of DK yarn in red (A) and
   green (B)
2.50mm (UK12:US-) crochet hook
Toy stuffing
Darning needle
1in (2.5cm) brooch bar

Size
Actual measurements:
2¾in (7cm) from tips of leaves to
   base of cherries

Tension
Not important

Method
The fruit is crocheted in continuous rounds. The leaves are worked in rounds using double crochet, half treble and treble stitches to form the shape. After stuffing the cherries, they are attached to the leaves with stalks in chain stitch, which are then slip stitched into.

Cherry (make 2)

Using 2.50mm hook and A, wind yarn round finger a couple of times to form a ring. Insert hook into ring, catch yarn and draw through, 1 ch (does not count as st).

Round 1: Work 6 dc into ring.

Round 2 (inc): (Dc2inc) 6 times (12 sts).

Round 3: 1 dc in each dc. Pull on short end of yarn to close ring.

Round 4 (inc): (Dc2inc) 12 times (24 sts).

Round 5: 1 dc in each dc.

Round 6 (dec): (Dc2dec) 12 times (12 sts).

Round 7 (dec): (Dc2dec, 1 dc) 4 times (8 sts).

Fasten off, leaving a long length of yarn. Stuff the cherry and run a gathering st around the opening, draw up and fasten off.

CHERRY

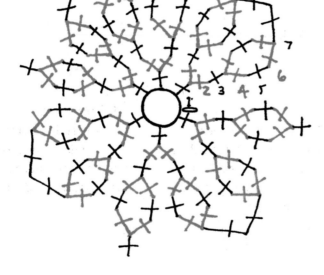

Leaf (make 2)

With 2.50mm hook and B, make 8 ch.

Round 1: 1 dc into 2nd ch from hook, 1 dc in next 5 ch, 3 dc in next ch, 1 dc down other side of foundation ch (15 sts).

Round 2: 3 ch, *1 dc in next dc, 1 htr in next dc, 1 tr in next 3 dc, 1 htr in next dc*, 1 dc in next 2 dc; rep from * to *, 1 dc in next dc, sl st into 3 ch sp. Fasten off and weave in ends.

LEAF

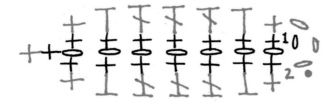

STALKS

Stalks

Row 1: With 2.50mm hook and B, work 1 dc into top, gathered end of first cherry, 4 ch, with RS facing work 1 dc into 3 ch sp of first leaf, with RS facing work 1 dc into 3 ch sp of next leaf, 4 ch, 1 dc into top of second cherry, turn.

Row 2: Sl st into each of next 4 ch of the stalk just made, sl st into the 2 dc joining the leaves, sl st in next 4 ch of the first stalk, finishing at the dc into the first cherry.
Fasten off.

Making up

Weave in ends. Join the leaves about a third of the way up to keep them in place. Attach a brooch bar to the back of the double leaf.

Variation: Cherry necklace

Make a delicate necklace using a 0.75mm (UK5:US12) crochet hook and crochet thread 20 in red (A) and green (B).

Cherry (make 2)

With 0.75mm hook and A, work to round 3 of cherry as given for cherry brooch.

Round 4 (inc): (Dc2inc, 1 dc) 6 times (18 sts).

Round 5: 1 dc in each dc.

Round 6 (dec): (Dc2dec) 9 times (9 sts).

Fasten off and stuff as for cherry brooch.

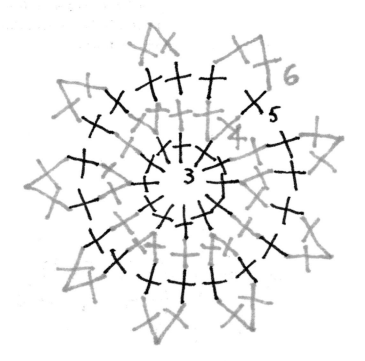

CHERRY ROUNDS 3–6

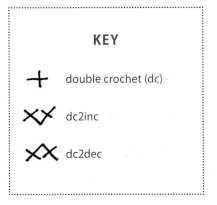

KEY

+	double crochet (dc)
✕✕	dc2inc
✕✕	dc2dec

Leaf (make 2)

With 0.75mm hook and B make 6 ch.

Round 1: 1 dc into 2nd ch from hook, 1 dc in next 3 ch, 3 dc in next ch, 1 dc down other side of foundation ch (11 sts).

Round 2: 2 ch, 1 dc in each dc, sl st into 2 ch sp. Fasten off and weave in ends.

Stalks

With 0.75mm hook and B, work row 1 of cherry stalks as for cherry brooch. Fasten off and weave in ends.

Loop

With 0.75mm hook and B, make 10 ch and join with a sl st to first ch to form a loop. Stitch securely between the two leaves so the loop faces forward.

Make a chain and fastening as given for Wild Strawberry (see pages 106–111) and attach the finished cherries.

KEY

⬯ chain (ch)

• slip stitch (sl st)

+ double crochet (dc)

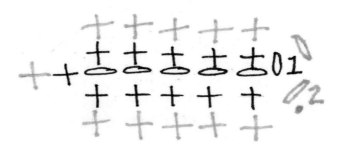

LEAF

Iced Doughnut

This jolly doughnut brooch is richly adorned with embroidered sprinkles scattered over pink crocheted icing, giving it that succulent, sticky look. Help yourself to a calorie-free treat!

Materials

Small amount of DK yarn in brown (A)

Small amount of 4ply yarn in pink (B)

Oddments of embroidery thread in various colours to decorate

2.50mm (UK12:US-) crochet hook

Small amount of toy stuffing

Darning needle

1¼in (3cm) brooch bar

Size

Actual measurements:

2½in (6.5cm) in diameter

⅞in (2.25cm) deep

Tension

Not important

Method

The chocolate base is worked first, beginning at the centre of the ring. The pink icing is started around the foundation chain of the doughnut base, and then continued in the same pattern. The open edges are joined by crocheting into both sets of stitches, stuffing the ring as you go. French knots decorate the iced top. Alternatively, seed beads can be stitched to the pink icing.

Chocolate base

Using 2.50mm hook and A, make 20 ch. Join with a sl st to first ch to form a ring.

Round 1: 1 ch (does not count as a st), work 1 dc into each ch (20 sts).

Round 2: 1 dc in each dc.

Round 3 (inc): (Dc2inc, 1 dc) 10 times (30 sts).

Rounds 4–5: 1 dc in each dc. Fasten off.

Icing

Round 1: Using 2.50mm hook and B and with RS of base facing, work 1 dc down reverse side of foundation chain (20 sts).

Rounds 2–4: Work rounds 3–5 as given for base. Do not fasten off.

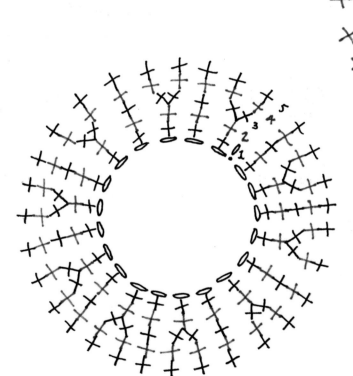

Foundation chain of Base

ICING

CHOCOLATE BASE

Making up

With base facing, WS tog and B, work 1 dc into each dc of the last round of both the base and the icing to join, stuffing the piece as you go. Embroider a number of French knots using the oddments of coloured yarns or threads to represent the sugar decorations. Sew brooch bar to the back of the doughnut.

KEY

 chain (ch)

• slip stitch (sl st)

+ double crochet (dc)

XX dc2inc

Fancy that!

Oya, the beautiful Turkish lace developed by Anatolian women, is believed to date back to the 8th century BC. A range of effects are created depending on the tool used, such as a crochet hook or sewing needle. The motifs often symbolize emotion or a stage in a woman's life.

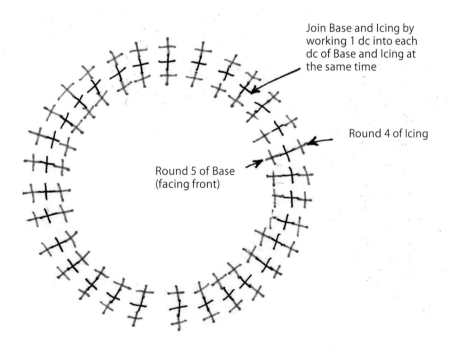

Join Base and Icing by working 1 dc into each dc of Base and Icing at the same time

Round 4 of Icing

Round 5 of Base (facing front)

MAKING UP

Handful of Sweeties

These flamboyant brooch designs echo the cornerstones of confectionery heaven: the humbug and the strawberry swirl. Wear them individually or a collection as a fanciful corsage.

Materials

Oddments of 4ply yarn in any shade for the main colour (A) and a contrast colour (B)
Small amount of silver metallic yarn (C)
2.50mm (UK12:US-) crochet hook
Toy stuffing
Darning needle
1in (2.5cm) brooch bar

Size

Actual measurements of round sweet:
1³⁄₈in (3.5cm) diameter excluding wrapper
3¹⁄₄in (8.25cm) across including wrapper
Actual measurements of humbug:
1³⁄₄in (4.5cm) across and 1in (2.5cm) wide excluding wrapper
3¹⁄₂in (9cm) across including wrapper

Tension

Not important

Method

The main part of the round sweet is worked in continuous rounds, changing colour each time to form the swirl. The striped humbug variation is crocheted in rows, alternating the contrasting colours. The wrapper is crocheted in various stitches to create the scalloped, decorative edge, then gathered at the narrow end and stitched to the sides of the sweet.

Sweet

Using 2.50mm hook and A, wind yarn around finger a few times to form a ring. Insert hook into ring, catch yarn and draw through, 1 ch (does not count as st).

Round 1: Work 5 dc into ring (5 sts).

Round 2 (inc): With B, (dc2inc) 4 times, 1 dc in next dc, change to A and work 1 dc in same dc as last st. Pull tightly on short end of A to close ring (10 sts).

Round 3 (inc): With A, (dc2inc, 1 dc) 4 times, dc2inc, change to B and work 1 dc in next dc (15 sts).

Round 4 (inc): With B, (dc2inc, 2 dc) 4 times, dc2inc, 1 dc, change to A and work 1 dc in next dc (20 sts).

Round 5 (inc): With A, (dc2inc, 1 dc) 9 times, dc2inc, change to B and work 1 dc in next dc (30 sts).

Round 6: With B, 1 dc in next 29 dc, change to A and work 1 dc in next dc.

Continue working in A:

Round 7: 1 dc in each dc.

Round 8 (dec): (Dc2dec, 1 dc) 10 times (20 sts).

Round 9: 1 dc in each dc.

Round 10 (dec): (Dc2dec, 2 dc) 5 times (15 sts).

Fasten off, leaving a long length of yarn.

KEY

⌒	chain (ch)
•	slip stitch (sl st)
+	double crochet (dc)
✕✕	dc2inc
⅄✕	dc2dec
⊤	half treble (htr)
Ŧ	treble (tr)
Ŧ	double treble (dtr)
◼	yarn A
◻	yarn B

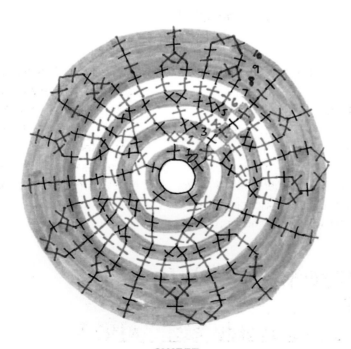

SWEET

Wrapper (make 2)

With 2.50mm hook and C, leaving a long length of yarn at the beginning, make 12 ch.

Row 1: 1 dc into 2nd ch from hook, 1 dc in next 10 ch, turn (11 sts).

Rows 2–3: 1 ch (does not count as a st), 1 dc in each dc, turn.

Row 4: 2 ch, (1 tr, 1 dtr, 1 tr, 1 htr) in first dc, *1 dc in next dc, (1 htr, 1 tr, 1 dtr, 1 tr, 1 htr) in next st; rep from * 4 more times, sl st to last dc of previous row and fasten off leaving a long length of yarn.

Making up

Stuff the sweet and run a gathering stitch around the opening, draw up and fasten off. Flatten the sweet and work a couple of stitches through the centre to keep its shape. Thread the long end of yarn through the foundation chain of the wrapper and draw up to gather. Fold the sweetie wrapper so the open ends meet at the centre back, stitch to secure the shape and attach to the side of the sweet. Repeat for the other side. Weave in loose ends. Sew the brooch bar to the back.

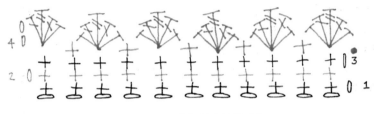

WRAPPER (MAKE 2)

Variation: Humbug

Make a striped humbug using contrasting colours of 4ply yarn in A and B.

With 2.50mm hook and A, make 11 ch.

Row 1 (WS): 1 dc in 2nd ch from hook, 1 dc in next 9 ch, turn (10 sts). Join in B.

Row 2: With B, 1 ch (does not count as a st), 1 dc in each dc, turn.

Row 3: As row 2 in B.

Rows 4–5: As row 2 in A.

Rep rows 2–5, alternating the colour as before to form stripes, until 15 rows have been worked.

With RS together and A, sl st into each of the back loops of every stitch of last row and foundation chain to join. Turn the work RS out, run a gathering st around one end, draw up and fasten off. Stuff the humbug, gather up the open end and fasten off.

Make the wrapper as given for the round sweet and finish off with a brooch bar.

Repeat until 15 rows complete

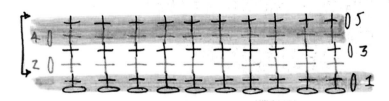

HUMBUG

Wild Strawberry

This scrumptious pendant evokes memories of the lazy days of summer all year round, with the succulent strawberry fruit highlighted by glistening embroidered seeds.

Materials

Oddments of 20 thread in red (A), green (B) and black (C)
Small amount of gold metallic thread
0.75mm (UK5:US12) crochet hook
Toy stuffing
Sewing needle

Size

Actual measurements:
$7/8$in (2.25cm) at widest part
$7/8$in (2.25cm) at longest part excluding loop

Tension

Not important

Method

The strawberry is worked in continuous rounds of double crochet and is similar to the heart patterns, although with less shaping to the top. The leafy stalk is formed with chain stitches that are slip stitched into, then attached to the top of the fruit, along with a short loop to hang from the necklace. Seeds are embroidered around the strawberry to decorate. The necklace is in chain stitch with a tiny crocheted button to fasten.

Strawberry

With 0.75mm hook and A, make 4 ch and join with a sl st to the first ch to form a ring. 1 ch (does not count as a st).

Round 1: 6 dc into ring (6 sts).

Round 2: 1 dc in each dc.

Round 3 (inc): (Dc2inc) 6 times (12 sts).

Round 4: 1 dc in each dc.

Round 5 (inc): (Dc2inc, 1 dc) 6 times (18 sts).

Round 6: 1 dc in each dc.

Round 7 (inc): (Dc2inc, 1 dc) 9 times (27 sts).

Round 8: 1 dc in each dc.

Round 9 (inc): (Dc2inc, 2 dc) 9 times (36 sts).

Rounds 10–12: 1 dc in each dc.

Shape top

Round 13: Work 1 dc in next 9 dc, turn, work 1 dc in each of opposite 9 dc to form half of top shaping (18 sts).

Round 14: 1 dc in each of the 18 dc just worked.

Fasten off and rejoin thread to the other side.

Rep last 2 rounds to match the first side. Fasten off.

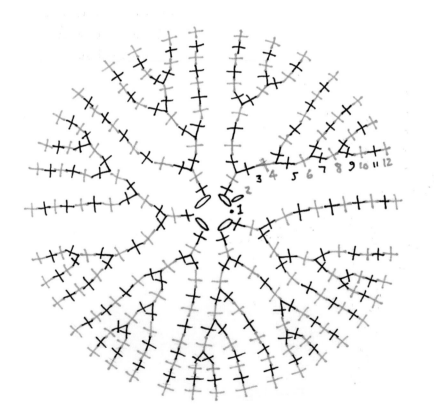

STRAWBERRY ROUNDS 1–12

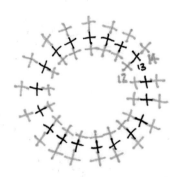

STRAWBERRY TOP-SHAPING ROUNDS 12–14

Leafy stalk

With 0.75mm hook and B, make 5 ch and join with a sl st to first ch to form a ring.

Next: (1 dc into ring, 6 ch, sl st into 2nd ch from hook, sl st into next 4 ch) 6 times, sl st into ring. Fasten off, leaving a long length of thread.

KEY

⬭ chain (ch)

✚ slip stitch (sl st)

• double crochet (dc)

✕✕ dc2inc

Fancy that!

It was the crop failures during the Irish potato famine of the 1840s and 1850s that forced farming families to look for alternative means of income such as producing crocheted items. Crocheted collars, cuffs and other accessories were much in demand by the upper classes.

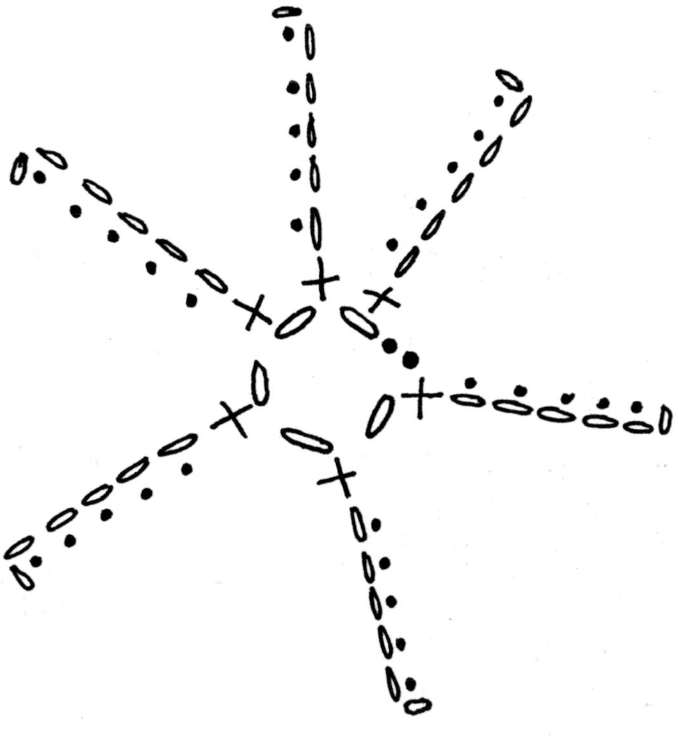

LEAFY STALK

Necklace

Button

Using 0.75mm hook and C, make 4 ch and join with sl st to first ch to form a ring.

Round 1: 1 ch (does not count as st), 6 dc into ring (6 sts).

Round 2 (inc): (Dc2inc) 6 times (12 sts).

Rounds 3–5: 1 dc in each dc. Fasten off leaving long length, thread through sts, stuff firmly, gather up and fasten off.

Chain and loop

Using 0.75mm hook and C, make 16 ch and join with sl st to first ch to form a ring.

1 ch, 24 dc into ring, sl st to first dc.

Next: Work a chain measuring 17in (43cm), or to desired length, allowing an extra $5/8$in (1.5cm) for attaching the strawberry.

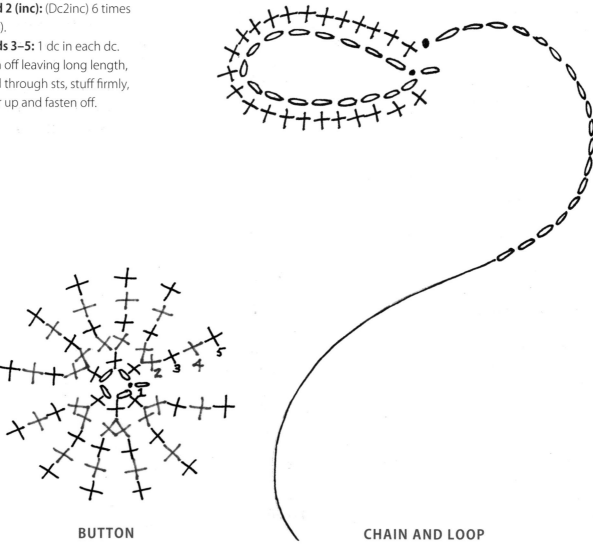

BUTTON　　　　**CHAIN AND LOOP**

Making up

Stuff the strawberry firmly. Gather half of top shaping to close the opening and fasten off neatly. Repeat for other side of shaping. Using the long length of thread, sew the leafy stalk to the top of the fruit, working a few stitches into the lower part of the leaves to hold them in place.

With 0.75mm hook and B, make 10 ch, sl st to first ch to form a loop. Fasten off and attach to centre of leaf. Embroider seeds around the strawberry by working a number of bullion stitches around the main part in gold metallic thread. Attach the crocheted chain to the strawberry by folding it in half and threading the doubled chain through the loop at the top of the stalk. Take the button and loop at the ends of the chain and thread them back through the folded necklace. Pull on the ends to tighten the chain.

Fancy that!

Irish crochet lace arrived in Italy in the early 20th century. In the town of Orvieto, Ars Wetana was founded, allowing the women to earn a modest income producing this new lace. A style of their own was soon developed, inspired by the reliefs in Orvieto cathedral.

KEY

⬯   chain (ch)

✚   slip stitch (sl st)

•   double crochet (dc)

✕✕   dc2inc

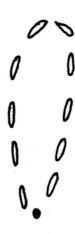

LOOP

111

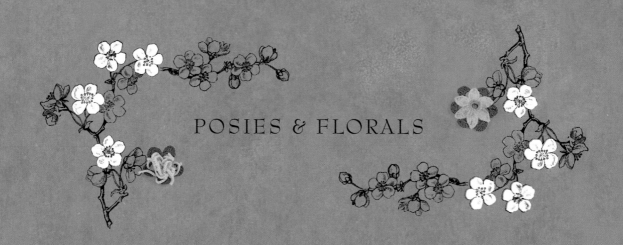

POSIES & FLORALS

Giant Poppy

With the use of textured yarns in striking colours and some shimmering sequins worked in to catch the light, this jolly oversized poppy hair adornment is guaranteed to turn heads!

Materials

Metallic yarn in black (A), 4ply yarn in a green-yellow shade (B) and pale pink or red (C)
2.50mm (UK12:US-) crochet hook
33 sequins
Small amount of toy stuffing
Length of hat elastic to fit head
Darning needle
Sewing needle
Sewing thread

Size

Actual measurements:
6in (15cm) across petals

Tension

Not important

Method

This very large bloom uses the long treble and double treble stitches to form the petals. The repetitive pattern around each petal makes this a great project with which to practise the more complicated stitches. The sequinned centre is worked first and attached to the petals to finish the poppy. A brooch bar can be sewn to the back of the flower to wear as a corsage.

Poppy centre

Thread 33 sequins on to yarn A. Using 2.50mm hook and A, wind yarn around finger a couple of times to form a ring. Insert hook into ring, catch yarn and draw through, 1 ch (does not count as st).

Round 1: 1 dc into ring, 3 ch (to count as first tr), 10 tr into ring, sl st in 3rd of 3 ch. Pull on short end of yarn to close ring (11 sts).

Join in B. Do not break off yarn A.

Rounds 2–3: 3 ch (to count as first tr), 1 tr in each tr, sl st in 3rd of 3 ch.

Round 4 (inc): With A, work 3 ch (to count as first tr), 1 tr in same st, (tr2inc) 10 times, sl st in 3rd of 3 ch, turn (22 sts).

Rounds 5–7: Working on WS, 3 ch (to count as first tr), (bring sequin to hook, 1 ch, 1 tr in next 2 tr) 10 times, sequin to hook, 1 ch, 1 tr in next tr, sl st in 3rd of 3 ch.

Round 8: 3 ch (to count as first tr), 1 tr in each tr, sl st in 3rd of 3 ch.

Round 9 (dec): 3 ch (to count as first tr), 1 tr in next tr, (tr2dec) 10 times, sl st in 3rd of 3 ch (12 sts).

Rounds 10–11: 3 ch (to count as first tr), 1 tr in each tr, sl st in 3rd of 3 ch. Fasten off, leaving a long length of both yarns.

Stuff the yellow centre and run a gathering stitch around the base where yarn A meets yarn B at round 4, draw up and fasten off. Gather the open end and push the yellow centre inside the sequinned black section, which will form a collar around the stuffed centre. Stitch in place by pushing the needle several times right through the work, from the gathered sequinned section to the metallic tip of the yellow centre.

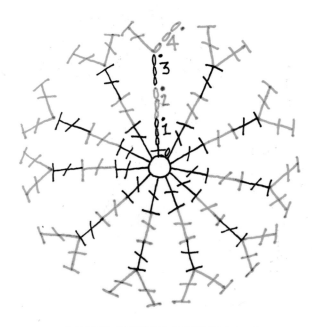

POPPY CENTRE ROUNDS 1–4

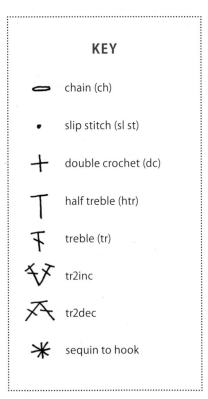

KEY

⬯	chain (ch)
•	slip stitch (sl st)
+	double crochet (dc)
T	half treble (htr)
⊤	treble (tr)
⋎	tr2inc
⋏	tr2dec
✳	sequin to hook

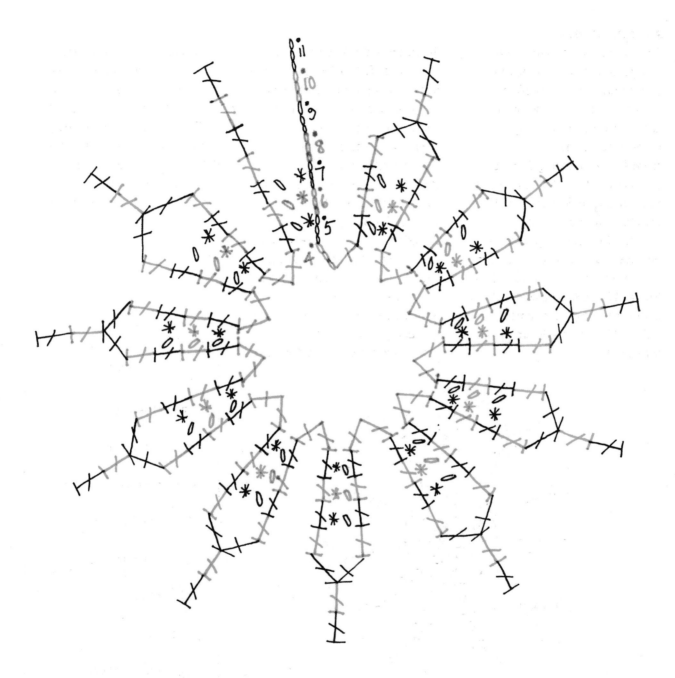

ROUNDS 4–11 (ROUNDS 5–11 ARE WORKED ON WS)

Petals

With 2.50mm hook and A, make 6 ch and join with a sl st to first ch to form a ring.

Round 1: 3 ch (to count as first tr), 2 tr into ring, (9 ch, 3 tr) 3 times, 9 ch, sl st to 3rd of 3 ch (12 tr and four 9 ch loops).

Round 2: (Miss next tr, 1 dc in next tr, miss next tr, (4 dc, 2 htr, 2 tr, 5 dtr, 2 tr, 2 htr, 4 dc) into next 9 ch loop) 4 times, sl st into first dc, sl st up next 4 dc of first petal. Change to yarn C.

Round 3 (inc): (1 htr in next 2 htr, 1 tr in next tr, (dtr3inc, dtr2inc) 3 times, dtr3inc, 1 tr in next tr, 1 htr in next 2 htr, miss next 4 dc down side of petal, miss 1 dc in between petals, miss 4 dc up side of next petal) 4 times (96 sts).

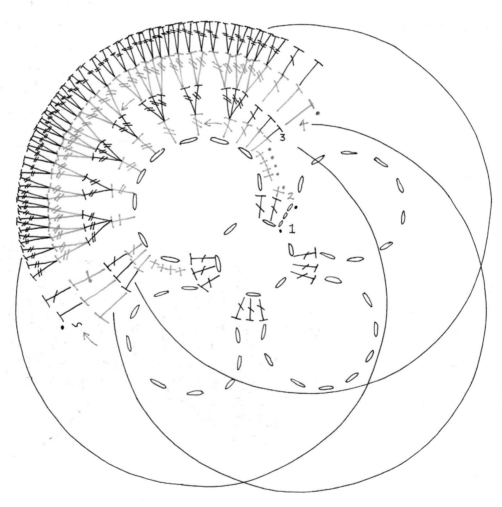

PETALS

Round 4 (inc): (1 htr in next 2 htr, 1 tr in next tr, dtr2inc in next 18 sts, 1 tr in next tr, 1 htr in next 2 htr) 4 times, sl st into next htr, turn (168 sts).

Round 5 (inc): Working on WS, (miss next htr, 1 htr in next htr, 1 tr in next tr, dtr2inc in next 36 sts, 1 tr in next tr, 1 htr in next htr, miss next htr) 4 times, sl st in next st (304 sts). Fasten off.

Making up

Attach centre of poppy to the middle of the petals on the RS. Weave in ends. Measure a length of hat elastic to fit around head and stitch to underside of poppy.

Fancy that!

The use of fascinators has long been seen in fashion history. French queen Marie Antoinette set fashion trends in the 18th century, often referencing current events. She once celebrated a French naval victory over the British by adorning her towering wig with a miniature ship.

KEY

⌒	chain (ch)
•	slip stitch (sl st)
✕	double crochet (dc)
T	half treble (htr)
⊤	treble (tr)
∓	double treble (dtr)
⩔	dtr2inc
⩙	dtr3inc

Daffodil

Bring spring to your wardrobe with this bright blossom headband. By replacing the band with a hairclip or brooch bar, this colourful accessory can be worn in a variety of ways.

Materials
Oddments of DK yarn in white (A), orange (B), green (C) and black (D)
Oddment of black metallic yarn (E)
3.00mm (UK11:USC2/D3) crochet hook
Darning needle

Size
Actual measurements:
4³⁄₈in (11cm) across leafy base

Tension
Not important

Method
The petals, trumpet, bead and the headband itself are all crocheted separately and stitched together to make up the finished piece. Various stitches are used to shape the petals. The band is worked in rows using treble stitches to create an open-weave fabric.

Petals

With 3.00mm hook and A, make 6 ch and join with a sl st to first ch to form a ring.

Round 1: (12 ch, 1 dc into 2nd ch from hook, 1 dc in next 10 ch, 2 dc into ring) 5 times, 12 ch, 1 dc into 2nd ch from hook, 1 dc in next 10 ch, 1 dc into ring (6 spokes).

Round 2: (Working into foundation ch, 1 dc into first ch, 1 htr in next ch, 1 tr in next 6 ch, 1 htr in next ch, 1 dc in next 2 ch, 1 ch, 1 dc in next 2 dc down other side of petal, 1 htr in next dc, 1 tr in next 6 dc, 1 htr in next dc, 1 dc in next dc) 6 times, sl st to first dc. Fasten off.

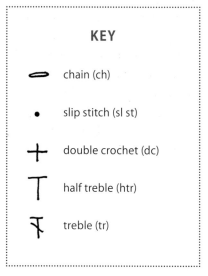

KEY

⌒	chain (ch)
•	slip stitch (sl st)
+	double crochet (dc)
T	half treble (htr)
⊤	treble (tr)

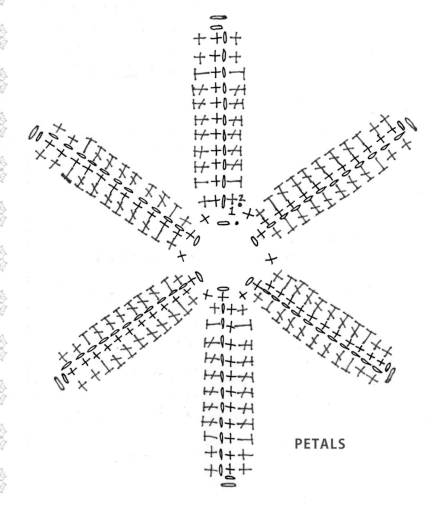

PETALS

Trumpet

With 3.00mm hook and B, leaving a long length of thread at the beginning, make 4 ch and join with a sl st to first ch to form a ring.

Round 1: 1 ch (does not count as a st), 7 dc into ring (7 sts).

Round 2 (inc): (Dc2inc) 7 times (14 sts).

Rounds 3–6: 1 dc in each dc.

Round 7 (inc): 3 ch (counts as first tr), 1 tr in same st, (tr2inc) 13 times, sl st to 3rd of 3 ch (28 sts). Fasten off.

Fancy that!

In Greek mythology, having rejected countless lovers, Narcissus fell in love with his own reflection in a pool of water. There he died and the white narcissus flower with its orange corolla grew from the earth where he lay.

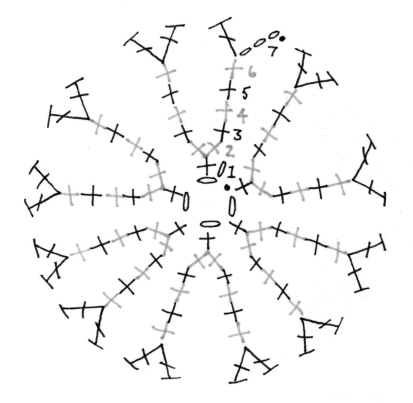

TRUMPET

KEY

⬭	chain (ch)
•	slip stitch (sl st)
+	double crochet (dc)
⊤	treble (tr)
✕✕	dc2inc
⋔	tr2inc

Leafy base

With 3.00mm hook and C, make 5 ch and join with a sl st to first ch to form a ring.

Round 1: 3 ch (to count as first tr), 11 tr into ring, sl st to 3rd of 3 ch (12 sts).

Round 2 (inc): 3 ch (to count as first tr), 1 tr in same st, (tr2inc) 11 times, sl st to 3rd of 3 ch (24 sts).

Round 3: 9 ch, miss 1 tr, (1 dc in next 3 tr, 8 ch, miss 1 tr) 5 times, 1 dc in next 2 tr (6 loops).

Round 4: (3 dc, 1 htr, 2 tr, 4 dtr, 2 tr, 1 htr, 3 dc) into each loop, sl st to first dc. Fasten off.

KEY

⬭   chain (ch)

•   slip stitch (sl st)

✕   double crochet (dc)

T   half treble (htr)

Ŧ   treble (tr)

⩔   tr2inc

Ŧ   double treble (dtr)

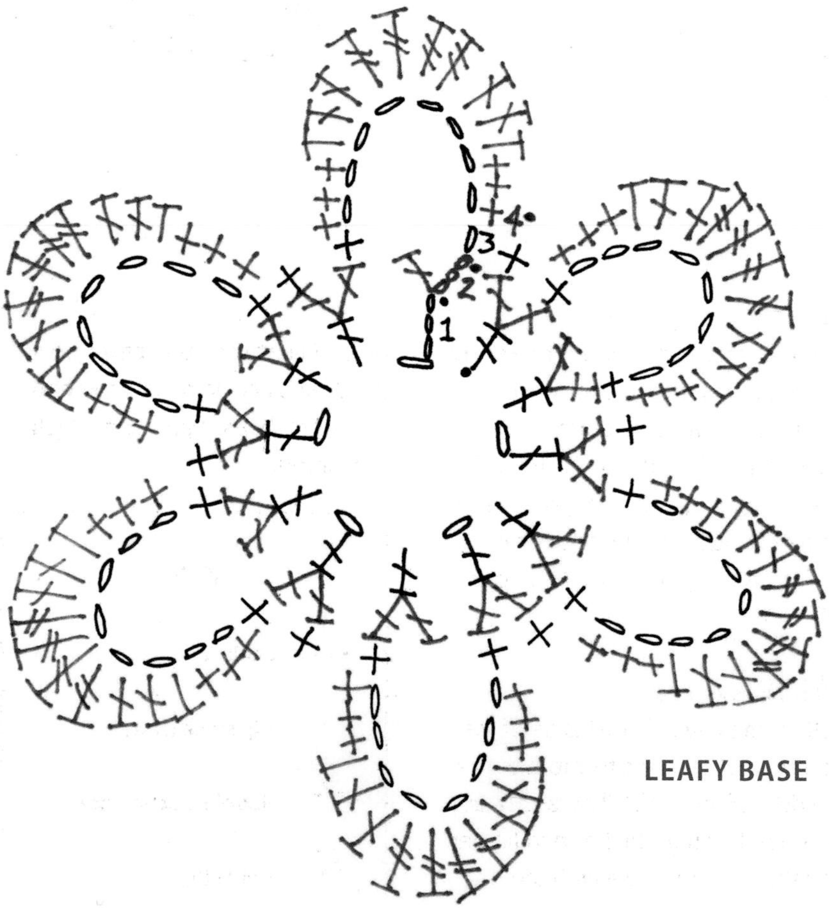

LEAFY BASE

HEADBAND

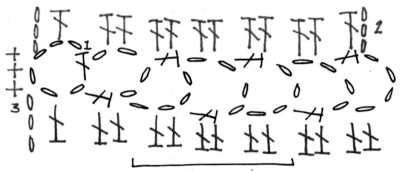

Repeat to required length

BEAD

Headband

With 3.00mm hook and D, make 6 ch.

Row 1: 1 tr into first ch to make first space, 4 ch, turn, 1 tr into 6 ch sp, *4 ch, turn, 1 tr into 4 ch sp; rep from * to make the required length to fit around head without stretching.

Row 2: 3 ch (to count as first tr), 1 tr in first 4 ch sp, 2 tr in all but last 6 ch sp, 1 tr in last 6 ch sp, 3 ch, 3 dc down side of last 6 ch sp.

Row 3: Working into opposite side of spaces, 3 ch (to count as first tr), 1 tr in first sp, 2 tr in each 4 ch sp to end. Fasten off.

Bead

With 3.00mm hook and E, make 5 ch and join with a sl st to form a ring.

Next: 3 ch, work 17 tr into ring, sl st to 3rd of 3 ch. Fasten off leaving a long length of yarn to run a gathering st around the outer edge, draw up to form a large bead. Fasten off.

Making up

Stitch the bead to the inside of the trumpet. Attach the trumpet to the middle of the daffodil petals. Weave in ends. Position the finished flower on the RS of the base with the petals in between the leaves. Sew neatly in place. Join the short ends of the crocheted band and attach the daffodil.

KEY

⌒	chain (ch)
•	slip stitch (sl st)
+	double crochet (dc)
⍅	treble (tr)

Pretty Posy

Inspired by a collection of vintage porcelain floral brooches, this posy of bright blooms is just as elegant. Delicacy is created in the use of fine cotton and metallic threads.

Materials

Oddments of 20 thread in white (A), yellow (B), blue (C), pink (D) and green (E)

Embroidery thread in metallic gold, using only two strands worked together (F)

0.75mm (UK5:US12) crochet hook

Sewing needle

1in (2.5cm) brooch bar

Size

Actual measurements:
2in (5cm) across leafy base

Tension

Not important

Method

Each flower is made and finished separately before being arranged on the leafy base. A variety of stitches is used in the pattern, including double crochet, half treble and treble. The gold centres of the periwinkle and daffodil are worked using gold embroidery thread, but a pretty bead can be stitched in place if preferred.

Daffodil petals

With 0.75mm hook and A, make 6 ch and join with a sl st to first ch to form a ring.

Round 1: (12 ch, sl st into 2nd ch from hook, sl st down next 10 ch, 2 dc into ring) 5 times, 12 ch, sl st into 2nd ch from hook, sl st down next 10 ch, 1 dc into ring.

Round 2: (Working into foundation ch, miss first ch, 1 dc in next ch, 1 htr in next ch, 1 tr in next 6 ch, 1 htr in next ch, 1 dc in next ch, 3 dc in end; working into back loops of sl sts,

1 dc in first sl st on other side of petal, 1 htr in next sl st, 1 tr in next 6 sl sts, 1 htr in next sl st, 1 dc in next sl st, miss next sl st) 6 times, sl st to first dc. Fasten off.

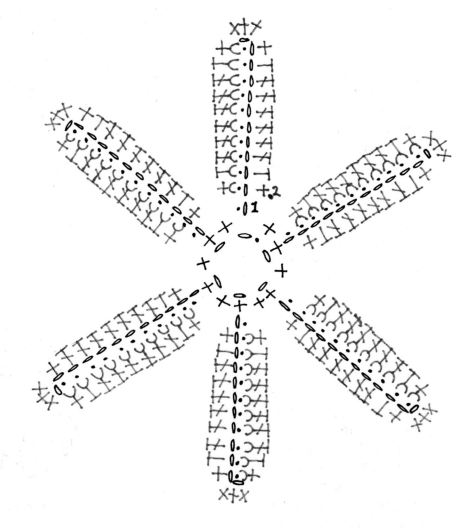

KEY

⌒ chain (ch)

• slip stitch (sl st)

+ double crochet (dc)

XX dc2inc

T half treble (htr)

T̄ treble (tr)

V̄ tr2inc

∩ into back loop

DAFFODIL PETALS

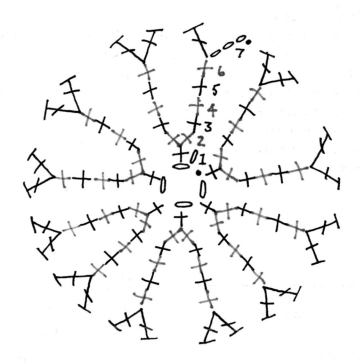

DAFFODIL TRUMPET

Daffodil trumpet

With 0.75mm hook and B, leaving a
long length of thread at the
beginning, make 4 ch and join with
a sl st to first ch to form a ring.
Round 1: 1 ch (does not count as a
st), 6 dc into ring (6 sts).
Round 2 (inc): (Dc2inc) 6 times
(12 sts).
Rounds 3–6: 1 dc in each dc.
Round 7 (inc): 3 ch (counts as first
tr), 1 tr in same st, (tr2inc) 11 times,
sl st to 3rd of 3 ch (24 sts).
Fasten off.

Daffodil bead

With 0.75mm hook and 2 strands of
F worked together, make 5 ch and
join with a sl st to form a ring.
Next: 3 ch, work 15 tr into ring, sl st
to 3rd of 3 ch. Fasten off, leaving a
long length of thread to run a
gathering st around the outer edge,
draw up and fasten off, creating a
little bead.

DAFFODIL BEAD

Periwinkle petals

With 0.75mm hook and B, make 6 ch and join with a sl st to first ch to form a ring.

Round 1: (12 ch, sl st into 2nd ch from hook, sl st down next 10 ch, 3 dc into ring) 4 times, 12 ch, sl st into 2nd ch from hook, sl st down next 10 ch, 2 dc into ring. Join in C.

Round 2: Work as given for round 2 of daffodil petals 5 times. Fasten off.

Periwinkle bead

Work as instructions for Daffodil Bead on page 129.

Work as instructions for Daffodil Bead on page 129.

KEY	
⊂⊃	chain (ch)
•	slip stitch (sl st)
+	double crochet (dc)
T	half treble (htr)
T	treble (tr)
⋎	tr2inc
∓	double treble (dtr)
∩	into back loop

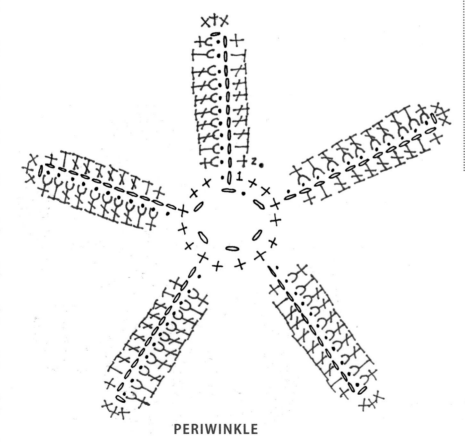

PERIWINKLE

Chrysanthemum

With 0.75mm hook and D, make 22 ch, sl st into 2nd ch from hook, sl st to end, turn, sl st into 2nd and 3rd sts.

Next: (18 ch, sl st into 2nd ch from hook, sl st into next 16 ch, turn, miss first st, sl st into next 2 sts) 19 times (20 petals).

Fasten off, leaving a long length of thread.

Leafy base

With 0.75mm hook and E, make 6 ch and join with a sl st to first ch to form a ring.

Round 1: 3 ch (to count as first tr), 13 tr into ring, sl st to 3rd of 3 ch (14 sts).

Round 2 (inc): 3 ch (to count as first tr), 1 tr in same st, (tr2inc) 13 times, sl st to 3rd of 3 ch (28 sts).

Round 3: 11 ch, miss 1 tr, (1 dc in next 3 tr, 10 ch, miss 1 tr) 6 times, 1 dc in next 2 tr (7 loops).

Round 4: (3 dc, 1 htr, 3 tr, 7 dtr, 3 tr, 1 htr, 3 dc) into each loop, sl st to first dc. Fasten off.

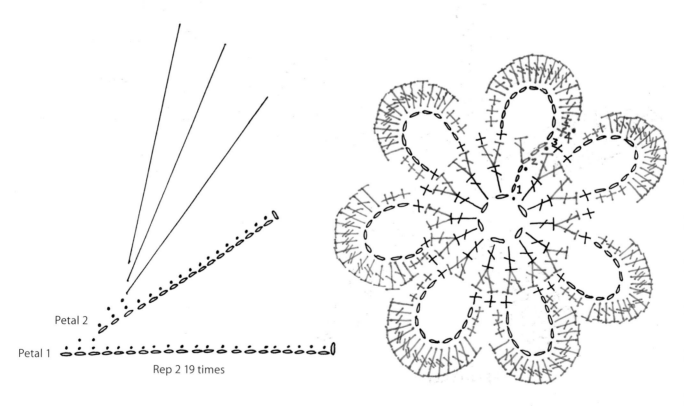

Petal 2

Petal 1

Rep 2 19 times

CHRYSANTHEMUM

LEAFY BASE

Making up

Sew the crocheted bead of the daffodil to the inside of the trumpet. Attach the trumpet to the centre of the petals. Sew the other crocheted bead to the centre of the periwinkle petals. Wind the chrysanthemum from the fastened-off end, keeping the base flat and stitching in place with the length of thread left. Twist the petals to curl. Starting with the periwinkle, sew each bloom to the base, stitching neatly through the petals to hold them in place. Weave in ends. Attach brooch bar to the back of the leafy base.

Variation: Single bloom brooches

Make the flowers to wear as a single bloom with a small leafy base to back them. Experiment with different shades of thread for an alternative look.

Daffodil leafy base

With 0.75mm hook and green thread, make 6 ch and join with a sl st to first ch to form a ring.

Round 1: 3 ch (to count as first tr), 11 tr into ring, sl st to 3rd of 3 ch (12 sts).

Round 2: 3 ch (to count as first tr), 1 tr in same st, (tr2inc) 11 times, sl st to 3rd of 3 ch (24 sts).

Round 3: 11 ch, miss 1 tr, (1 dc in next 3 tr, 10 ch, miss 1 tr) 5 times, 1 dc in next 2 tr (6 loops).

Round 4: (3 dc, 1 htr, 3 tr, 7 dtr, 3 tr, 1 htr, 3 dc) into each loop, sl st to first dc. Fasten off.

Stitch the finished flower neatly to the base with the petals positioned in between the leaves. Attach a small brooch bar to the back.

DAFFODIL LEAFY BASE

Periwinkle and chrysanthemum leafy base

With 0.75mm hook and green thread, make 5 ch and join with a sl st to first ch to form a ring.

Round 1: 3 ch (to count as first tr), 9 tr into ring, sl st to 3rd of 3 ch (10 sts).

Round 2: 3 ch (to count as first tr), 1 tr in same st, (tr2inc) 9 times, sl st to 3rd of 3 ch (20 sts).

Round 3: 11 ch, miss 1 tr, (1 dc in next 3 tr, 10 ch, miss 1 tr) 4 times, 1 dc in next 2 tr (5 loops).

Round 4: (3 dc, 1 htr, 3 tr, 7 dtr, 3 tr, 1 htr, 3 dc) into each loop, sl st to first dc. Fasten off.

Finish as for daffodil base, with the chrysanthemum petals curled into shape as before.

Fancy that!

The Victorians covered their homes and clothing in crochet after the craft's promotion at London's Great Exhibition in 1851. Trimmings for fashions and household accessories were in great demand.

KEY

- ⬭ chain (ch)
- • slip stitch (sl st)
- ✚ double crochet (dc)
- ⊤ half treble (htr)
- ⊤ treble (tr)
- ⋎ tr2inc
- ⊤ double treble (dtr)

PERIWINKLE AND CHRYSANTHEMUM LEAFY BASE

Delicate Poppy

By using a fine thread, the petals of this dainty crocheted poppy brooch will feel almost as delicate as the real thing. A thicker thread will produce a more compact, sturdier fabric.

Materials

Crochet thread 20 in black (A), yellow (with optional lime-green metallic machine embroidery thread worked together) (B)
Crochet thread 40 or 20 in red or pink (C)
0.75mm (UK5:US12) crochet hook
Tiny amount of toy stuffing
Sewing needle
1in (2.5cm) brooch bar

Size

Actual measurements:
2½in (6.5cm) across

Tension

Not important

Method

A similar pattern to the Giant Poppy (see page 115), this delicate version uses the long crochet stitches and very fine thread to form the papery quality of poppy petals. The yellow centre is filled with a tiny amount of stuffing, and the black cotton thread surrounding it is folded back on itself and stitched in place.

Poppy centre

With 0.75mm hook and A, make 4 ch and join with a sl st to the first ch to form a ring.

Round 1: 3 ch (to count as first tr), 10 tr into ring, sl st to 3rd of 3 ch. Do not break thread (11 sts). Join in B.

Rounds 2–3: 3 ch (to count as first tr), 1 tr in next 10 tr, sl st to 3rd of 3 ch.

Round 4 (inc): With A, work 3 ch (to count as first tr), 1 tr in same st, (tr2inc) 10 times, sl st to 3rd of 3 ch (22 sts).

Rounds 5–9: With A, 3 ch (to count as first tr), 1 tr in each tr, sl st to 3rd of 3 ch.

Fasten off, leaving a long length of thread in A and B. Stuff the yellow-green centre piece and gather the base where B ends and A begins at round 4. Draw up and fasten off.

Run a gathering st around the edge of the final round and push the yellow centre towards the gathered end so it sits inside the surrounding black. Stitch the gathered black end to the yellow inner, working the stitches right through from the base to the centre top. Pliers may come in handy here to help coax the needle through the stuffed piece.

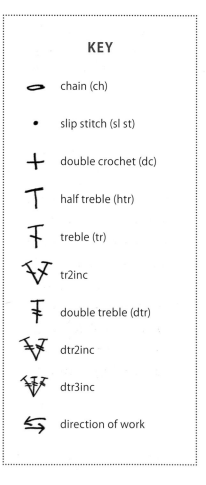

KEY

⬭	chain (ch)
•	slip stitch (sl st)
+	double crochet (dc)
T	half treble (htr)
⊤	treble (tr)
V	tr2inc
⊤	double treble (dtr)
V	dtr2inc
V	dtr3inc
↰	direction of work

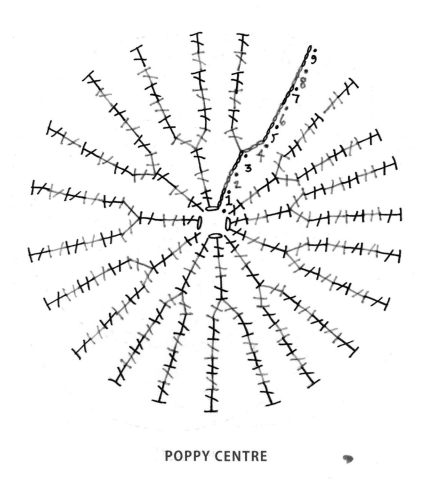

POPPY CENTRE

Poppy petals

With 0.75mm hook and A, make 6 ch and join with a sl st to form a ring.

Round 1: 3 ch (to count as first tr), 2 tr into ring, (9 ch, 3 tr) 3 times, 9 ch, sl st to 3rd of 3 ch (12 tr and four 9 ch loops).

Round 2: (Miss next tr, dc into next tr, miss next tr, (4 dc, 2 htr, 2 tr, 5 dtr, 2 tr, 2 htr, 4 dc) into next 9 ch loop) 4 times, sl st into first dc. Sl st into next 4 dc of first petal. Join in C.

Round 3: (1 htr in next 2 htr, 1 tr in next tr, (dtr3inc, dtr2inc) 3 times, dtr3inc, 1 tr in next tr, 1 htr in next 2 htr, miss next 4 dc down side of petal, miss dc in between petals, miss next 4 dc of next petal) 4 times (96 sts).

Round 4 (inc): (1 htr in next 2 htr, 1 tr in next tr, dtr2inc in next 18 sts, 1 tr in next tr, 1 htr in next 2 htr) 4 times, sl st to first htr of next petal, turn (168 sts).

Round 5 (inc): Working on the WS of the petals, (miss next htr, 1 htr in next htr, 1 tr in next tr, dtr2inc in next 36 sts, 1 tr in next tr, 1 htr in next htr, miss next htr) 4 times, sl st to first htr. Fasten off (304 sts).

Making up

Attach centre of poppy to the middle of the petals on the RS. Stitch a brooch bar to the back.

Fancy that!

In the early 20th century there came another lull in the passion for crochet. Crocheted trimmings lost their appeal with the development of the sewing machine, which brought about ease and speed in producing clothing.

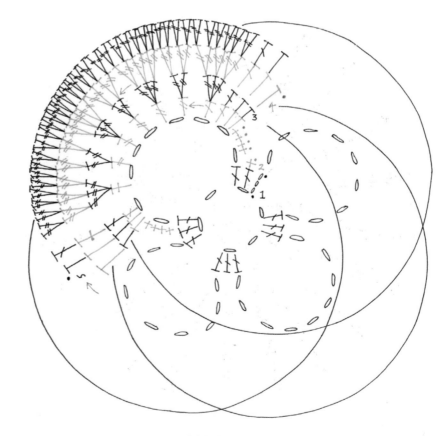

POPPY PETALS

SMALL TREASURES

Charms

The ancient tradition of adorning a simple chain with trinkets is the inspiration for this project. Here modern icons decorate a pretty crocheted bracelet with an adjustable fastening.

Materials

Oddments of 4ply yarn in 5 colours
   (A, B, C, D and E), oddment of 4ply
   yarn in contrast shade for heart (F)
Metallic yarn for chain and leaves (G)
2.50mm (UK12:US-) crochet hook
Sewing thread
9 x sequins
1 x ⅛in (4mm) pearl bead
8 –10 x seed beads
1 x faceted bead
1 x head pin
Toy stuffing
Darning needle
Sewing needle
Round-nose pliers
Cutting pliers

Size

Actual measurements:
Length 8in (20cm)

Tension

Not important

Method

Each charm and leaf is made individually, using a variety of stitches and simple increasing and decreasing to form the shaping. The ribbed pattern of the cupcake case is made by crocheting into the horizontal loop below that of the normal loop of the stitch to be worked. Beads and sequins decorate the charms which, along with the leaves, are attached to the chain as it is crocheted.

Bag

Using A and 2.50mm hook, make 4 ch, join with sl st to first ch to form a ring.

1 ch (does not count as st), 9 dc into ring.

Row 1: 1 dc into first 5 dc, turn, (5 sts). This forms the flap of the bag and buttonhole.

Row 2: 1 ch (does not count as st), 1 dc in each of next 5 dc, 5 ch, sl st to first dc to join.

The following is worked in rounds:

Round 3: 1 dc in each of the 5 ch just worked, 1 dc in each of the 5 dc across bag flap (10 sts).

Round 4: 1 dc in each dc.

Round 5 (inc): Dc2inc, 3 dc, (dc2inc) twice, 3 dc, dc2inc (14 sts).

Round 6: 1 dc in each dc.

Round 7 (inc): Dc2inc, 5 dc, (dc2inc) twice, 5 dc, dc2inc (18 sts).

Round 8: 1 dc in each dc.

Next: Fold work and sl st tog the back loops of 9 sts on each side of bag to join. Fasten off.

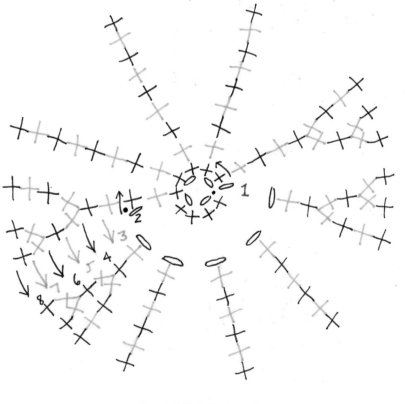

BAG ROUNDS 1–8

KEY

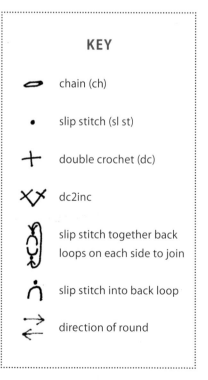

⬯	chain (ch)
•	slip stitch (sl st)
✚	double crochet (dc)
✕	dc2inc
	slip stitch together back loops on each side to join
	slip stitch into back loop
↔	direction of round

Decorative edging and handle

With back of bag facing, join in B at right hand corner of opening where the straight edge meets the bag flap, sl st into back loops of each dc over flap, sl st into opposite corner of opening, make 10 ch, sl st to first corner to form the bag handle. Fasten off and weave in ends.

Sequin fringe

Thread 9 sequins onto sewing thread doubled, and with 2.50mm hook and back of bag facing, join to the back loops of sl st at lower edge, sequin to hook, 1 ch, 1 dc into first st, (sequin to hook, 1 ch, 1 dc into next st) 8 times. These stitches will be loose due to the fine thread and larger hook, allowing the sequins to move freely and catch the light. Fasten off and weave in ends. Sew a 4mm pearl bead to the straight edge, under the flap, for the button. Button up the bag.

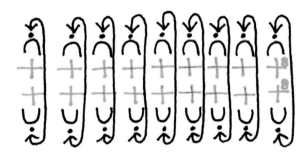

BAG ROUNDS 8 AND NEXT

Start edging here

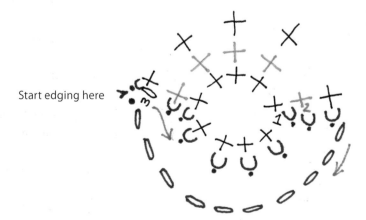

DECORATIVE EDGING AND HANDLE

143

Hat

Crown

Using C and 2.50mm hook, wind yarn around finger a couple of times to form a ring. Insert hook, catch yarn and draw through ring, 1 ch (does not count as st).

Round 1: 7 dc into ring (7 sts).
Round 2 (inc): (Dc2inc) 7 times (14 sts). Pull on short end of yarn to close ring.
Rounds 3–4: 1 dc in each dc.
Rounds 5–6: Join in A and rep rounds 3 and 4.

Brim

Round 7: With C, sl st to next dc, 2 ch, 1 htr in same place as sl st, (htr2inc) 13 times, sl st to 2nd of 2 ch ensuring yarn A is at the front of the work (28 sts). Fasten off C and leave A attached.

Curly ribbons

Insert hook at the start of round 5 in A, round the back of the stitch and out through the front, catch the length of yarn still attached and draw through the st, *11 ch, 2 dc in 2nd ch from hook, (sl st in next ch, 2 dc in next ch) 4 times, sl st in next ch, sl st into hat*. Rep from * to *. Fasten off and weave in ends. Twist each ribbon into shape.

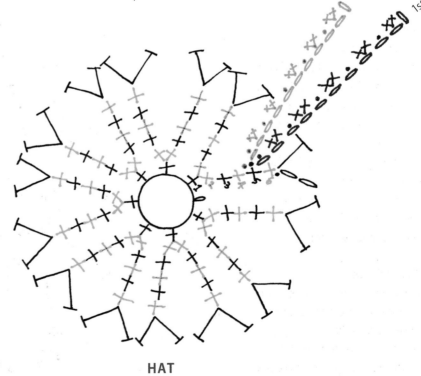

2nd ribbon

1st ribbon

HAT

KEY

⬭	chain (ch)
•	slip stitch (sl st)
+	double crochet (dc)
⋎⋎	dc2inc
T	half treble (htr)
V	htr2inc

Shoe

Sole

Using D and 2.50mm hook, *make 4 ch and join with sl st to first ch to form ring.

Round 1: 1 ch (does not count as st), 9 dc into ring (9 sts).

Round 2: 7 ch, 1 dc into 2nd ch from hook, 1 dc into next 5 ch, 1 dc into next 9 dc, 1 dc down reverse side of 6 ch (21 sts). Fasten off and weave in ends.*

Insole

Using C and 2.50mm hook, rep from * to *.

Upper

Round 3: Place the soles with WS together and the sole facing front. Using B and 2.50mm hook, begin at the start of the widest part (the toe) and work 1 dc through all loops of 21 dc to join.

Round 4: 1 dc in each dc, finishing at the start of the toe.

Round 5: (Miss 1 dc, 1 dc in next dc) 4 times, sl st to next st. Fasten off and weave in loose ends.

Edging and laces

Round 6: Insert 2.50mm hook from the inside at centre front of shoe, catch yarn E and draw through, leaving a long length to tie into a bow. With RS facing, sl st into back loops only of each dc to the centre back of the heel, 5 ch, sl st into same place as last sl st, inserting the hook through the last sl st as well to form loop, sl st into each dc to centre front of shoe. Fasten off leaving a long length for the bow. Tie lengths of yarn into a double bow. Trim ends. Paint a tiny amount of PVA glue on ends to prevent them fraying.

KEY

⟳	chain (ch)
•	slip stitch (sl st)
+	double crochet (dc)
∩	slip stitch into back loop
➤	start round here

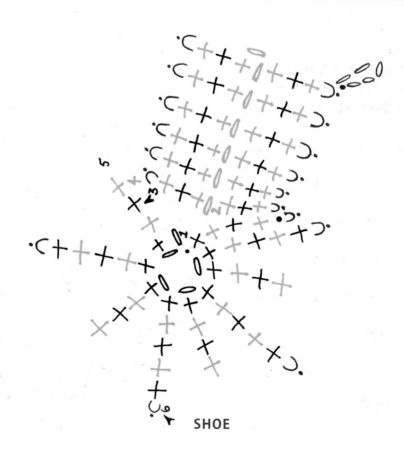

SHOE

Heart

Using F and 2.50mm hook, wind yarn around finger a couple of times to form a ring. Insert hook, catch yarn and draw through ring, 1 ch (does not count as st).

Round 1: 5 dc into ring (5 sts).

Round 2: 1 dc in each dc, pull on short end of yarn to close the ring.

Round 3 (inc): (Dc2inc) 5 times (10 sts).

Round 4: 1 dc in each dc.

Round 5 (inc): (Dc2inc) 10 times (20 sts).

Round 6: 1 dc in each dc.

Shape top

Round 7: 1 dc in next 5 dc, turn, 1 dc in opposite 5 dc to form first side of top of heart shape (10 sts).

Round 8: 1 dc in each of 10 dc. Rejoin yarn to remaining 10 sts and work 2 rounds of 1 dc in each st to match other side of heart.

Break yarn and stuff heart. Work running st around the top of first side, gather up and fasten off. Finish other side of top shaping to match the first.

Thread a bead onto a head pin and poke through the tip of the heart. Use round-nose pliers to curl the wire and trim with cutting pliers.

KEY

⬭   chain (ch)

•   slip stitch (sl st)

✚   double crochet (dc)

✕✕   dc2inc

⊕   double crochet into horizontal loop below loop of stitch on previous row

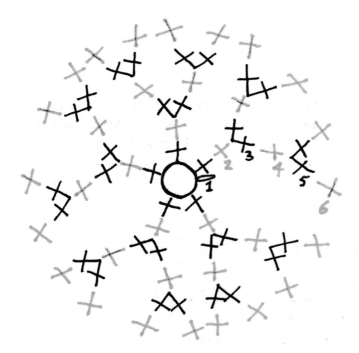

HEART ROUNDS 1–6

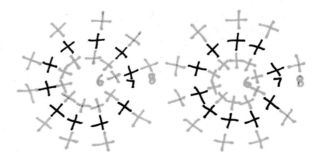

HEART TOP-SHAPING ROUNDS 6–8

Cupcake

Cake

Using E and 2.50mm hook, wind
yarn around finger a couple of times
to form a ring. Insert hook, catch
yarn and draw through ring, 1 ch
(does not count as st).

Round 1: 5 dc into ring (5 sts).

Round 2: 1 dc into each dc. Pull
on short end of yarn to close ring.

Round 3 (inc): (Dc2inc) 5 times
(10 sts).

Rounds 4–7: 1 dc in each dc.
Break yarn, thread through rem sts,
stuff the cake, gather up and fasten
off. Weave in ends.

CAKE

Cake case

Using D and 2.50mm hook, make
5 ch that will form the side seam
rather than the lower edge.

Row 1: 1 dc into 2nd ch from hook,
1 dc in next 3 ch, turn (4 sts).

Row 2: 1 ch (does not count as st),
1 dc in each of the horizontal loops
that lay below the loop of the dc on
previous row, turn (see photograph
left). Rep row 2 until work fits snugly
around the cake.

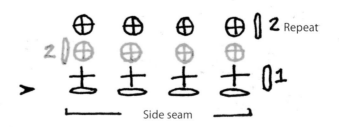

CAKE CASE

Cake base

Using D and 2.50mm hook, make 4 ch, join with sl st to first ch to form a ring.

Round 1: 1 ch (does not count as st), 5 dc into ring (5 sts).

Round 2: Dc2inc (5 times), sl st to next st (10 sts).

Fasten off. Join seam of cake case and stitch around cake. Attach base to the case. Sew a scattering of seed beads over the top for decoration.

Leaves (make 6)

Using G and 2.50mm hook, make 8 ch.

Round 1: 1 dc into 2nd ch from hook, 1 dc into next 5 ch, 3 dc in end ch, 1 dc down reverse side of foundation ch (15 sts).

Round 2: 3 ch, *1 dc in next dc, 1 htr in next dc, 1 tr in next 3 dc, 1 htr in next dc,* 1 dc in next 2 dc, rep from * to *, 1 dc in next dc, sl st to next st. Fasten off and weave in ends.

CAKE BASE

KEY	
⬯	chain (ch)
•	slip stitch (sl st)
+	double crochet (dc)
T	half treble (htr)
⊤	treble (tr)
Ⅹ	dc2inc

Making up

Using G and 2.50mm hook, make 10 ch, join with sl st to first ch to form a loop.

9 ch, with top of shoe facing, work 1 dc into 5 ch loop at the heel to join, *sl st into 2nd and 3rd ch from hook, 5 ch, with RS facing, join in leaf with 1 dc into 3 ch sp, sl st into 2nd and 3rd ch from hook, 5 ch*, with top of hat facing, work 1 dc into edge of brim to join, rep from * to *, join heart with 1 dc into one side of top shaping, rep from * to *, with front of bag facing, work 1 dc into 10 ch sp to join, rep from * to *, join cupcake with 1 dc into side of cake, rep from * to *.

Next: 1 ch, join in final leaf with 1 dc into 3 ch sp, sl st back along each ch, including the 10 ch forming the loop at the beginning. Fasten off and weave in ends. Pull leaves into shape. The bracelet size can be altered by crocheting more or fewer stitches between the charms and leaves.

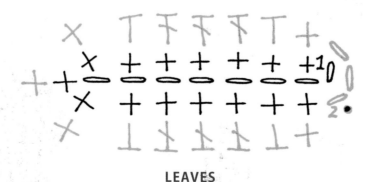

LEAVES

Variation: Alternative cupcake case

Here is a simple alternative rib pattern for the cake case.
Using D and 2.50mm hook, make 5 ch that will form the side seam rather than the lower edge.

Row 1: 1 dc into 2nd ch from hook, 1 dc in next 3 ch, turn (4 sts).
Row 2: 1 ch (does not count as st), 1 dc in back loops only of each dc, turn.

Rep row 2 until work fits snugly around the cake. Finish as given for the cupcake pattern.

<table>
<tr><td>

KEY

⬯	chain (ch)
+	double crochet (dc)
+⌒	double crochet into back loop

</td></tr>
</table>

Repeat

ALTERNATIVE CUPCAKE CASE

Variation: Keyrings

Simply attach a keyring to the charms.

Heart Icon

This project brings together an intricate heart motif with a straightforward band to make a pretty ring. Gold thread running through the band adds a touch of glamour.

Materials

Crochet thread 10 in black and gold
   metallic (A), pale pink (B)
1.25mm (UK3:US8) crochet hook
Tiny amount of toy stuffing
Sewing needle

Size

Actual measurements:
Heart measures $7/8$in (2.25cm) at
   widest point and $7/8$in (2.25cm) at
   longest point
Band measures $1/2$in (1.25cm) deep

Tension

Not important

Method

The band is a simple filet design worked in rows and joined at the seam. The heart is made in continuous rounds of double crochet, increasing the stitches to give shape. This ring is crocheted on a larger hook than the other small-scale projects.

Band

With 1.25mm hook and A, make
6 ch.

Row 1: 1 tr into first ch to make first
space, 4 ch, turn, 1 tr into 6 ch sp, *4
ch, turn, 1 tr into 4 ch sp; rep from *
to make the required length to fit
around finger loosely, as the
finished piece will be tighter.

Row 2: 2 ch (to count as first htr), 1
htr in first 4 ch sp, 2 htr in all but last
6 ch sp, 1 htr in last 6 ch sp, 2 ch, 3
dc down side of last 6 ch sp.

Row 3: Working into opposite side
of spaces, 2 ch (to count as first htr),
1 htr in first sp, 2 htr in each 4 ch sp
to end. Fasten off.

Heart

With 1.25mm hook and B, wind yarn
around finger a couple of times to
form a ring. Insert hook into ring,
catch yarn and draw through, 1 ch
(does not count as st).

Round 1: Into ring work 5 dc (5 sts).

Round 2: 1 dc in each dc.

Round 3 (inc): (Dc2inc) 5 times. Pull
on short end of thread to close ring
(10 sts).

Round 4: 1 dc in each dc.

Round 5 (inc): (Dc2inc, 1 dc) 5 times
(15 sts).

Round 6: 1 dc in each dc.

Round 7 (inc): (Dc2inc, 2 dc) 5 times
(20 sts).

Round 8: 1 dc in each dc.

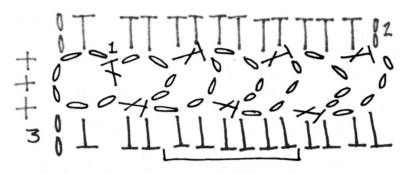

Repeat to required length

BAND

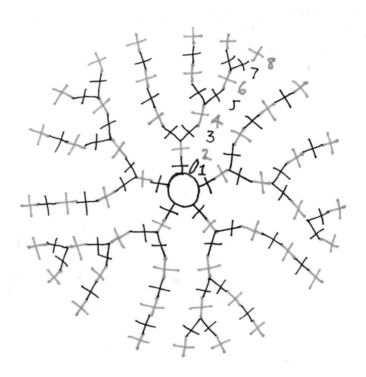

HEART ROUNDS 1–8

Shape top

Round 9: 1 dc in next 5 dc, turn, 1 dc in opposite 5 dc to form first side of top shaping (10 sts).

Round 10: 1 dc in each dc.

Fasten off, leaving a long length of thread to finish top.

Rejoin thread to remaining sts and work rounds 9 and 10 to match first side of shaping.

Making up

Stuff the heart firmly, using the end of the crochet hook to push the stuffing down. Run a gathering st around each opening, then draw up to close and fasten off. Weave in ends. Join the short ends of the band and stitch the heart over the seam.

KEY

⬭	chain (ch)
•	slip stitch (sl st)
✚	double crochet (dc)
✕✕	dc2inc
⊤	half treble (htr)
⊤	treble (tr)

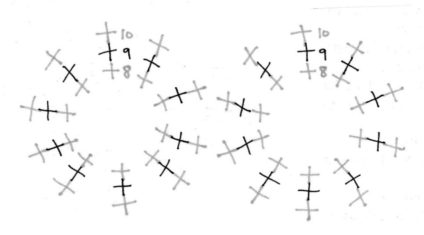

TOP-SHAPING ROUNDS 8–10

Oak Leaf & Acorn

This sculptural piece of nature's bounty makes a subtle and elegant pendant, further enhanced by the contrast of the roundedness of the acorn to the flatness of the oak leaf.

Materials

Crochet thread 20 in rich dark
    brown (A) and green (B)
Very fine wool or 2ply embroidery
    yarn in light brown (C)
0.75mm (UK5:US12) crochet hook
Tiny amount of toy stuffing
Sewing needle
PVA glue

Size

Actual measurements:
Acorn is ¾in (2cm) long
Oak leaf is 1in (2.5cm) long

Tension

Not important

Special abbreviations

Tr3tog: Work 3 tr together: (yrh, insert hook into st, yrh, draw back through st, yrh, draw through 2 sts) 3 times (4 loops on hook), yrh, draw through all loops on hook.

Method

The nut and acorn cups are finished separately and joined by a crocheted chain, which is slip stitched into to finish the stalk. Various stitches are used to shape the oak leaf. The empty cup and leaf are given a coating of PVA glue to stiffen the fabric and keep the shape. The necklace consists of a tiny crocheted nut and loop at each end of a chain to fasten. The acorn and leaf are separate pieces, but are threaded to hang together from the necklace.

Acorn nut

With 0.75mm hook and A, make 4 ch and join with a sl st to first ch to form a ring.

Round 1: 1 ch (does not count as a st), 9 dc into ring (9 sts).

Round 2 (inc): (Dc2inc) 9 times (18 sts).

Rounds 3–9: 1 dc in each dc. Fasten off leaving a long length of thread. Stuff the nut and run a gathering st around the opening, draw up to close and fasten off.

Acorn hat

With 0.75mm hook and C, make 5 ch and join with a sl st to first ch to form a ring.

Round 1: 1 ch (does not count as a st), 10 dc into ring (10 sts).

Round 2 (inc): (Dc2inc) 10 times (20 sts).

Rounds 3–6: 1 dc in each dc. Sl st to next st. Fasten off and stitch securely over the gathered end of the nut.

Empty cup

Work as for the acorn hat to the end of round 2.

Rounds 3–5: 1 dc in each dc.

Round 6: Sl st into back loops of each dc.

Fasten off.

Stalk

With 0.75mm hook and C, work 1 dc into the top of the acorn hat, 9 ch, 1 trtr into the top of the empty cup, 15 ch, sl st into the 10th ch from hook to form a loop, sl st into each of the ch, sl st into the first dc. Fasten off and weave in ends.

KEY

⬯	chain (ch)
•	slip stitch (sl st)
+	double crochet (dc)
XX	dc2inc
⊤	triple treble (trtr)
⌣	slip stitch into back loop

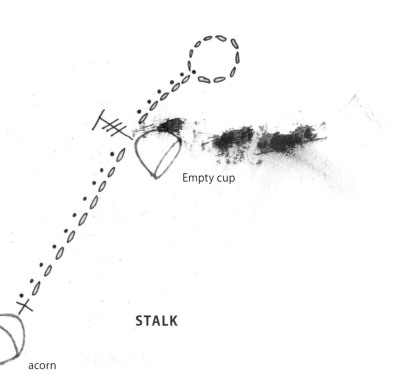

Empty cup

STALK

acorn

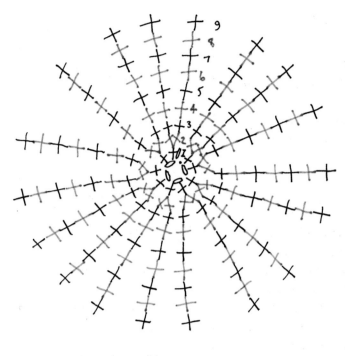

ACORN NUT

EMPTY CUP

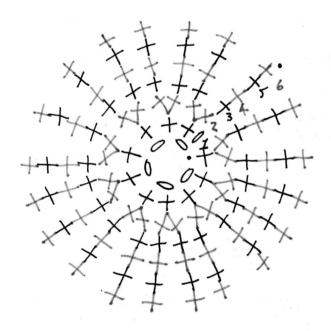

ACORN HAT

Oak leaf

With 0.75mm hook and B, make
19 ch.
Sl st into 2nd ch from hook, sl st into
next 17 ch.

Shape first side

Working down reverse side of ch, sl
st into first st, (1 dc in next st, 1 htr in
next st, 1 tr in next st, 4 ch, 1 dc into
2nd ch from hook, 1 htr in next ch,
1 tr in next ch, 1 dc in same st as
the 1 tr before the 4 ch shaping,
miss 2 ch) 3 times.

Shape top

1 dc in next st, 1 htr in next st,
1 ch, tr3tog in end, 1 ch; working
in back loops of sl sts, 1 htr in
next st, 1 dc in next st.

Shape other side

(Miss 2 ch, 1 dc in next st, 4 ch, 1 dc
in 2nd ch from hook, 1 htr in next
ch, 1 tr in next ch, 1 tr in same st as
the 1 dc before the 4 ch shaping, 1
htr in next st, 1 dc in next st) 3 times,
sl st to next st, 10 ch, sl st to first ch
to form a loop. Fasten off and weave
in ends.

Necklace nut button

With 0.75mm hook and A, make
4 ch and join with a sl st to form
a ring.

Round 1: 1 ch (does not count as a
st), 6 dc into ring (6 sts).

Round 2 (inc): (Dc2inc) 6 times
(12 sts).

Rounds 3–6: 1 dc in each dc.
Fasten off, stuff and gather top to
close. Weave in ends.

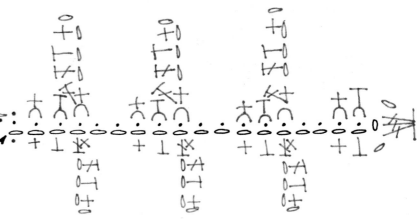

OAK LEAF

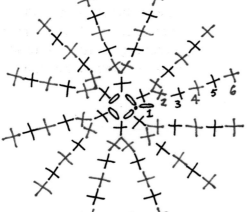

NECKLACE NUT BUTTON

Loop and chain

With 0.75mm hook and A, make 16 ch and join with a sl st to first ch to form a loop.

Next: 1 ch, 24 dc into loop, sl st to first dc. Make a chain measuring 17in (43cm), or to desired length, allowing an extra ⅝in (1.5cm) for attaching the acorn. Fasten off and sew nut button to end.

Making up

Paint the inside of the empty cup and the back of the oak leaf with PVA glue and leave to dry completely. Fold the chain in the middle to form a loop. Insert a crochet hook through the loop on the acorn stalk and the leaf, catch the folded chain and draw it through. Pass the ends of the necklace through the looped chain. Pull tightly on ends to secure.

KEY	
⬭	chain (ch)
•	slip stitch (sl st)
+	double crochet (dc)
XX	dc2inc
T	half treble (htr)
⊤	treble (tr)
⋔	tr3tog
⌒	slip stitch into back loop

LOOP AND CHAIN

Variation

Make the leaf using cotton 20 thread in autumnal shades, or two strands of gold metallic embroidery thread for an alternative finish.

159

Triangle & Heart

This striking cufflink set brings the playful poetry of wearing your heart on your sleeve to life. Combining a maker's dedication and affection it makes a perfect creative gift.

Materials

Crochet thread 20 in black (A) and
   red (B)
0.75mm (UK5:US12) crochet hook
Tiny amount of toy stuffing
Sewing needle

Size

Actual measurements:
The triangles measure ⁵⁄₈in (1.5cm)
   on each side
The heart is ⁵⁄₈in (1.5cm) at the
   longest part and ⁵⁄₈in (1.5cm) at
   the widest
The little bead is just over ⁵⁄₈in
   (1.5cm) long

Tension

Not important

Method

The triangles are formed in continuous rounds of double crochet, which are padded out with a little toy stuffing then joined by slip stitching the stitches together at the top edge. The tiny bead and heart are also in double crochet, worked in continuous rounds. A short foundation chain in doubled thread links the two pieces of each cufflink.

Triangle (make 2)

With 0.75mm hook and A, make 4 ch and join with a sl st to first ch to form a ring.

Round 1: 1 ch (does not count as a st), 5 dc into ring (5 sts).

Round 2 (inc): (Dc2inc) 5 times (10 sts).

Round 3: 1 dc in each dc.

Round 4 (inc): (Dc2inc, 1 dc) 5 times (15 sts).

Rounds 5–6: 1 dc in each dc.

Round 7 (inc): (Dc2inc, 2 dc) 5 times (20 sts).

Rounds 8–10: 1 dc in each dc.

This will form a cone shape. Do not fasten off. Stuff the shape, but do not over stuff. Sl st together the back loops of each side of the opening to join and form the triangle. Fasten off and weave in ends.

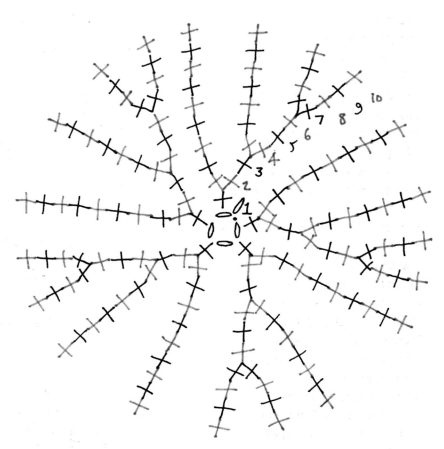

TRIANGLE

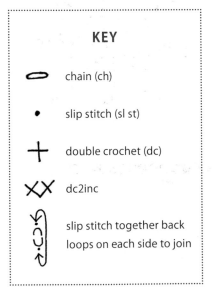

KEY

◯ chain (ch)

• slip stitch (sl st)

+ double crochet (dc)

XX dc2inc

slip stitch together back loops on each side to join

sl st tog back loops to join

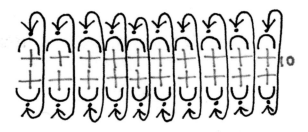

LINK

Heart

With 0.75mm hook and B, make
4 ch and join with a sl st to first ch
to form a ring.

Round 1: 1 ch (does not count as
a st), 6 dc into ring (6 sts).

Round 2 (inc): (Dc2inc) 6 times
(12 sts).

Rounds 3–4: 1 dc in each dc.

Round 5 (inc): (Dc2inc, 2 dc) 4 times
(16 sts).

Rounds 6–7: 1 dc in each dc.

Shape top

Round 8: 1 dc in next 4 dc, turn,
1 dc in opposite 4 dc to form first
side of top shaping (8 sts).

Rounds 9–10: 1 dc in each dc.
Fasten off leaving a long length of
thread to finish top.

Rejoin thread to other side and work
3 rounds of 1 dc in each of the
remaining 8 dc to match the first
side of top shaping.

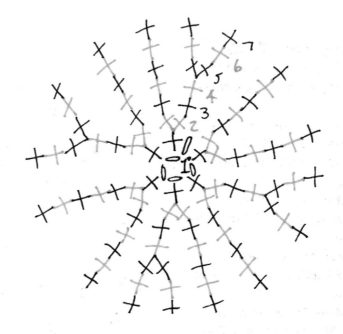

HEART ROUNDS 1–7

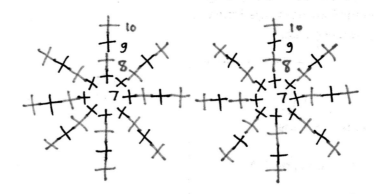

HEART TOP-SHAPING ROUNDS 7–10

Bead

With 0.75mm hook and A, make
4 ch and join with a sl st to form
a ring.

Round 1: 1 ch (does not count as
a st), 5 dc into ring (5 sts).

Round 2 (inc): (Dc2inc) 5 times,
(10 sts).

Rounds 3–10: 1 dc in each dc. The
work tends to curl inside out on the
first few rounds, so use the end of
the crochet hook to help turn the
RS out on the 3rd or 4th round.
Fasten off, leaving long length
of thread.

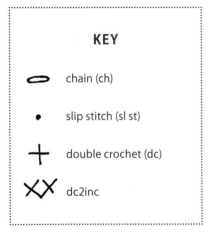

KEY

⬭ chain (ch)

• slip stitch (sl st)

+ double crochet (dc)

✕✕ dc2inc

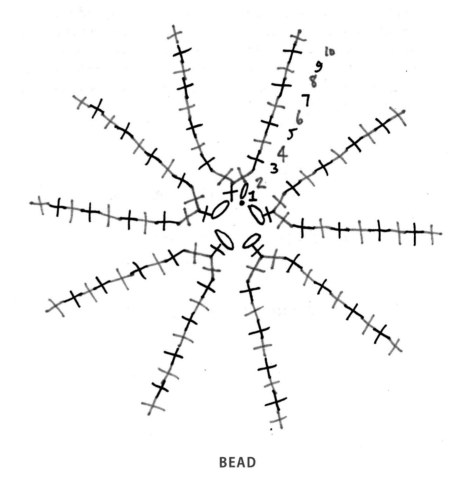

BEAD

Making up

Stuff the bead firmly, using the other end of the crochet hook to push the stuffing down. Gather the open end, draw up and fasten off. Stuff the heart, but not too firmly as it may not fit through the buttonhole if it is over-stuffed. Run a gathering stitch around the top opening, draw up and fasten off. Repeat on other side of shaping.

Link

With 0.75mm hook and A doubled, work 1 dc into the middle of the length of the bead, 7 ch, fasten off, leaving a long length of thread to stitch the link to the triangle. Weave in remaining ends. Repeat for the other cufflink, working the dc into the centre of the back of the heart.

Bead or heart

LINK (USE THREAD DOUBLED)

Fancy that!

Rather than being restricted to using traditional cotton, other materials can be incorporated into crochet. Vivienne Westwood's Ethical Fashion Africa collection featured recycled materials to produce beautiful crochet pieces handcrafted by women in Kenya.

Mod Targets

Capturing the iconic imagery of youth and rebellion in 1960s Britain, these target cufflinks are an impressive gift that can easily be adapted to a tie pin for the matching set!

Materials
Crochet thread 20 in red (A), white (B) and blue (C)
0.75mm (UK5:US12) crochet hook
Tiny amount of toy stuffing
Sewing needle

Size
Actual measurements:
Target measures just over ⅝in (1.5cm) in diameter
Bead measures ¾in (1.75cm) long

Tension
Not important

Method
The main pieces are worked in continuous rounds of double crochet, joining in the colours and increasing the stitches to form the front of the target design. The stitches are then decreased to shape the back and continued in blue thread. The beads are made separately and the pieces joined with a foundation chain using doubled thread.

Target (make 2)

Leaving a long length of thread at the beginning, with 0.75mm hook and A, make 4 ch and join with a sl st to first ch to form a ring.

Round 1: 1 ch (does not count as a st), 6 dc into ring, sl st to first dc (6 sts).

Round 2 (inc): Join in B, (dc2inc) 6 times (12 sts)

Round 3 (inc): (Dc2inc, 1 dc) 6 times, sl st to first dc (18 sts).

Round 4 (inc): Join in C, (dc2inc, 1 dc) 9 times (27 sts).

Rounds 5–7: 1 dc in each dc.

Round 8 (dec): (Dc2dec, 1 dc) 9 times (18 sts).

Round 9 (dec): (Dc2dec, 1 dc) 6 times (12 sts).

Fasten off leaving a long length of C.

Bead (make 2)

With 0.75mm hook and C, make 4 ch and join with a sl st to form a ring.

Round 1: 1 ch (does not count as a st), 5 dc into ring (5 sts).

Round 2 (inc): (Dc2inc) 5 times, (10 sts).

Rounds 3–10: 1 dc in each dc. Fasten off, leaving long length of thread.

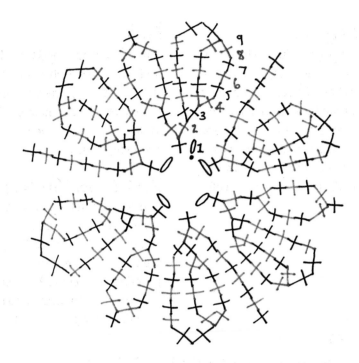

TARGET

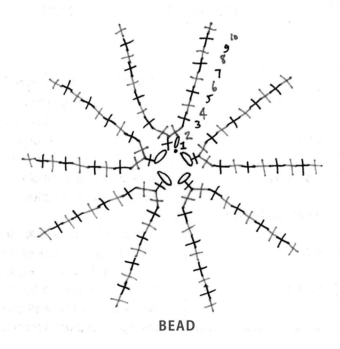

BEAD

Making up

Stuff the target. With the length of A left at the beginning, work a few stitches from the centre through the stuffing and back again to flatten the shape. Gather the opening and draw up to close. Weave in ends. Stuff the bead firmly and gather the open end, draw up and fasten off. Weave in ends.

Link

With 0.75mm hook and C doubled, work 1 dc into middle of the length of the bead, 7 ch, fasten off leaving a long length of thread to stitch the link to the target. Weave in remaining ends.

Variations: Target pin

Work as for target from rounds 1 to 6, and rounds 8 to 9. Stuff the shape as for cufflinks, inserting a flat-plated pin before gathering up to close. Add a clutch back to the pin to secure it to the wearer's clothing.

Fancy that!

The Royal Air Force's target roundel was first seen on British aircraft during World War II. Taken from the design of the French gunners in World War I, the symbol became a fashion icon of the mods in the 1960s, along with scooters and sharp suits.

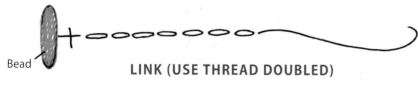

Bead

LINK (USE THREAD DOUBLED)

KEY

 chain (ch)

• slip stitch (sl st)

✛ double crochet (dc)

✕✕ dc2inc

✕✕ dc2dec

Variations: Target keyring

This is a suitable project for a beginner. It uses oddments of 4ply yarn in red (A), white (B) and blue (C), a 2.50mm (UK12:US-) crochet hook, a small amount of stuffing, a keyring and some pliers.

With 2.5mm hook and A, wind yarn around finger a couple of times to form a ring, leaving a long length of yarn at the beginning. Insert hook into ring, catch yarn and draw through, 1 ch (does not count as st).

Work rounds 1 to 9 of the target pattern, pulling on the long end left at the beginning of A to close the ring before finishing off as for target, making just one. Using the pliers, attach the keyring to the side of the target.

Suppliers

Yarns and threads

AUSTRIA
PaperPhine
Froebelgasse 33/10
1160 Vienna
office@paperphine.com
www.paperphine.com

FRANCE
Renaissance Dyeing
Andie Luijk
Le Fort
09300, Lieurac
Ariège
Tel: +33 (0) 5 61 05 27 60
www.renaissancedyeing.com

JAPAN
Avril
26 Asatsuyugahara-cho
Kamigamo, Kita-ku
Kyoto 603-8035
Tel: +81(0) 75 702 9406
www.avril-kyoto.com

NEW ZEALAND
South Seas Knitting
20 Livingstone Street
Auckland 1022
Tel: +64 (0) 9 3601 188
www.southseasknitting.com

UK
Appleton Brothers Ltd
Thames Works
Church Street
London W4 2PE
Tel: +44 (0) 20 8994 0711
www.embroiderywool.co.uk

Coats Crafts UK
Green Lane Mill
Holmfirth
West Yorkshire
HD9 2DX
Tel: +44 (0) 1484 681881
www.coatscrafts.co.uk

Jamieson & Smith
90 North Road
Lerwick
Shetland ZE1 0PQ
Tel: +44 (0) 1595 693579
www.shetlandwoolbrokers.co.uk

DMC
DMC Creative World Limited
Unit 21 Warren Park Way
Warrens Park
Enderby
Leicester
LE19 4SA
Tel: +44 (0) 116 275 4000
www.dmc.com

USA
Habu Textiles
135 West 29th Street
Suite 804
New York, NY 10001
Tel: +1 212 239 3546
www.habutextiles.com

Crochet hooks

UK

Deramores
Units 5–9 Tomas Seth Business Park
Argent Road
Queenborough ME11 5TS
Tel: +44 (0) 845 519 4573
www.deramores.com

HobbyCraft Group Limited
7 Enterprise Way
Aviation Park
Bournemouth International Airport
Christchurch
Dorset BH23 6HG
Tel: +44 (0) 1202 596100
www.hobbycraft.co.uk

USA

Stitch Diva Studios
848 N. Rainbow Blvd. #688
Las Vegas, NV 89107
www.stitchdiva.com

Haberdashery

UK

Ernest Wright and Son Limited
Endeavour Works
58 Broad Lane
Sheffield S1 4BT
Tel: +44 (0)114 273 9977
www.ernestwright.co.uk

MacCulloch & Wallis
25–26 Dering Street
London W1S 1AT
Tel: +44 (0)20 7629 0311
www.macculloch-wallis.co.uk

Ray Stitch
99 Essex Road
London N1 2SJ
Tel: +44 (0)20 7704 1060
www.raystitch.co.uk

USA

Purl Soho
459 Broome Street
New York, NY 10013
Tel: +1 212 420 8796
www.purlsoho.com

Beads, Findings & Jewellery Tools

UK

Beads Unlimited
PO Box 1
Hove, East Sussex BN3 3SG
Tel: +44 (0)1273 740777
www.beadsunlimited.co.uk

The Brighton Bead Shop
21 Sydney Street
Brighton, East Sussex BN1 4EN
Tel: +44 (0)1273 675077

**The Bead Shop
(Nottingham) Limited**
7 Market Street
Nottingham NG1 6HY
Tel: +44 (0)115 9588 899
www.mailorder-beads.co.uk

Kernowcraft Rocks & Gems Limited
Bolingey
Perranporth
Cornwall
TR6 0DH
Tel: +44 (0) 1872 573888
www.kernowcraft.com

References

Vintage needlework books are an amazing source of historical reference, especially those published during World War I and II, emphasizing 'make do and mend' and clever use of materials.

Books

The Lady's Crochet-Book
by Elvina Mary Corbould
London: Hatchards, Piccadilly, 1878

Encyclopedia of Needlework
by Thérèse de Dillmont
DMC Library, Brustlein & Co, 1884

Practical Knitting Illustrated
by Margaret Murray
and Jane Koster
Odhams Press Ltd, 1940

The Complete Book of Crochet
by Elizabeth L. Mathieson
The World Publishing Company, 1946

Elizabeth Craig's Needlecraft
Collins, 1947

Golden Hands Encyclopedia of Knitting and Crochet
Marshall Cavendish Ltd, 1973

A Complete Guide to Crochet
Edited by Pam Dawson
Marshall Cavendish Books Ltd, 1981

Websites

www.encyclopediaofneedlework.com

www.crochetinsider.com

www.heirloomcrochet.com

Abbreviations

ch = chain
cm = centimetre(s)

dc = double crochet
dc2dec = double crochet 2 stitches together to decrease
dc2inc = 2 double crochet stitches into next stitch to increase
dec = decrease
dtr = double treble
dtr2inc = 2 double trebles into next stitch to increase
dtr3inc = 3 double trebles into next stitch to increase

htr = half treble
htr2inc = 2 half trebles into next stitch to increase

in = inch(es)
inc = increase

mm = millimetre(s)

rem = remaining
rep = repeat
RS = right side

sl st = slip stitch

sp = space
st(s) = stitch(es)

tog = together
tr = treble
tr2dec = treble 2 stitches together to decrease
tr2inc = 2 treble stitches into next stitch to increase
trtr = triple treble

WS = wrong side

yrh = yarn round hook

Conversions

UK/US crochet terms

UK	US	
Double crochet	Single crochet	
Half treble	Half double crochet	
Treble	Double crochet	

UK	US	
Double treble	Triple crochet	
Triple treble	Double triple crochet	

About the author

Vanessa Mooncie is a contemporary crochet jewellery designer and maker, as well as silkscreen artist and illustrator. Her crocheted pieces are intensely detailed and fine in their execution using new and vintage yarns, threads and semi-precious stones. Vanessa's designs and creativity are inspired by the rich tradition of knit and crochet through the history of fashion, and are a synthesis of modern approaches to design and style through sourcing and researching traditional handcraft techniques.

Vanessa's experience includes studying fashion and textile design, and a self-employed career as a children's wear designer, illustrator and commercial interior designer.

She currently works in a rural English village on the South Downs in Sussex, an area that inspires her business and creativity.

Dedication

For Damian, Miriam, Dilys, Flynn, Honey and Dolly

Acknowledgements

I would like to thank my late grandmother, Eva Deadman, and my mother, Brenda Born, for patiently teaching me to crochet when I was little. Thank you to Damian, my lovely husband, for supporting and encouraging my creativity and to my children for their endless enthusiasm and excitement for my work. Thank you to all who have inspired me.

Index

To order a book or to request a catalogue, please contact:

GMC Publications, Castle Place, 166 High Street,
Lewes, East Sussex BN7 1XU, United Kingdom
Tel: +44 (0)1273 488005 Fax: +44 (0)1273 402866

www.gmcbooks.com

AWESOME!

CONTENTS

THE 'KISS OF DEATH'
ASSASSIN BUG
- PAGE 8

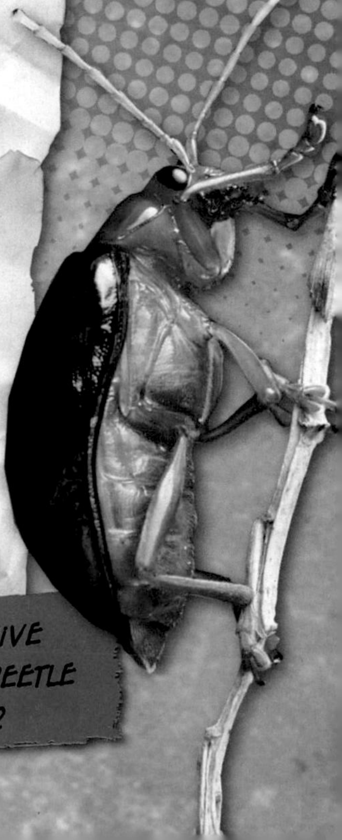

THE EXPLOSIVE
BOMBARDIER BEETLE
- PAGE 12

THE SUPER NATURAL WORLD OF BUGS

Welcome to the supernatural world of bugs. This book will take you on an amazing journey to meet some of the world's weirdest and most wonderful minibeasts. Are you ready for the ride?

Every day, we use five key senses – sight, sound, smell, touch, and taste – as we go about our daily lives. Our brains process this information so we can make sense of the world and communicate with others. Bugs and minibeasts have their own ways of sensing the world. Some have sharper sight, stronger smell, super-sensitive touch, or even senses that are completely outside our own experience – so much so that they appear to be supernatural powers!

SUPER SIGHT

Vision helps many bugs find food, move around, and hide from predators. Some bugs have far sharper eyesight than our own and can see things much more clearly. Others see the world completely differently, sensing forms of light that are invisible to the human eye.

FINELY TUNED

Many different bugs have a remarkable sense of hearing and can detect the faintest noises. Others can pick up sounds outside the human range of hearing.

SMELL AND TASTE

Our own smell and taste are weak compared to those of many bugs. A sharp sense of smell helps them to find food, pick up the scent of mates, avoid enemies or sniff their way through unfamiliar places.

SKIN DEEP

Some bugs live in complete darkness all the time – for example, in caves or under the ground. Good eyesight is useless in the dark, so instead these bugs have developed super-sensory touch to feel their way around. Some even have special touch organs, such as antennae and feelers, to help them move around in safety.

SUPER NATURAL POWER!

There are some bugs that have developed incredible supernatural powers outside our own experience. Can you imagine being able to regenerate new arms and legs or freeze solid for months? Some bug superpowers are just plain amazing – such as the ability to boil an enemy alive or spray it with toxic chemicals.

LOOK OUT FOR THESE SPECIAL FEATURES!

CRITTER STATS!

You can find out the key information about each bug in this box feature, such as its typical size, how many species (different types) there are in its group, and in what type of habitat the bug lives.

MEANWHILE, AT THE MOVIES...
SUPERHERO STYLE

GET READY TO MEET SOME OF THE COMIC-BOOK CHARACTERS AND ANIMATED ACTION HEROES (AND VILLAINS!) THAT SHARE THE SUPERNATURAL POWERS OF THE BUGS IN THIS BOOK. FIND OUT ABOUT EVERYTHING FROM THE CRYOGENIC SUPERPOWERS OF MR FREEZE TO THE INCREDIBLE REGENERATIVE POWERS OF WOLVERINE.

THE HUMAN FACTOR

THIS BOX WILL EXPLORE SOME OF THE WAYS IN WHICH SCIENTISTS HAVE HARNESSED THE SUPERPOWERS OF BUGS AND MINIBEASTS IN SCIENCE, TECHNOLOGY, MEDICINE AND OTHER AREAS TO MAKE OUR LIVES MUCH EASIER.

THE MIND-CONTROLLING ANT-DECAPITATING FLY

Ant-decapitating flies would be your worst nightmare – if you were a fire ant! These fearsome flies lay their eggs inside the bodies of the ants. When the eggs hatch, the maggots eat the ants from the inside out, eventually munching their way through the victims' brains and turning them into zombie ants!

There are around 110 species of ant-decapitating flies. These fearsome flies live in tropical parts of South America in the same places as the fire ants. Ant-decapitating flies have also been introduced to other parts of the world, including the United States, to control the exploding populations of ants.

CRITTER STATS!

Size: Up to 5 mm
Number of species: 110
Habitat: Tropical South America

THE HUMAN FACTOR

SCIENTISTS CALLED FORENSIC ENTOMOLOGISTS USE THE MAGGOTS OF SOME FLIES TO HELP CONVICT MURDER SUSPECTS. SOME FLIES LAY THEIR EGGS ON HUMAN CORPSES. THE ENTOMOLOGISTS MEASURE THE SIZE AND DEVELOPMENT OF THE MAGGOTS TO DETERMINE HOW LONG THEY HAVE BEEN ALIVE. THIS CAN THEN BE USED TO ESTIMATE THE TIME OF A PERSON'S DEATH.

SUPER NATURAL POWER!

Ant-decapitating flies have the **supernatural power of mind control,** but they achieve this feat in a horribly gruesome way. The female flies constantly buzz around the ant colony, looking for a suitable host. She then jumps on the ant, **stabs it with her ovipositor,** and lays an egg inside its body. When the egg hatches, the maggot starts to eat its way through the body of the ant and into its head. Eventually, the growing maggot **munches through the living ant's brain**, effectively turning it into a zombie.

AWESOME!
THIS PICURE SHOWS AN EGG IN A FEMALE FLY'S OVIPOSITOR, SEEN THROUGH AN ELECTRON MICROSCOPE.

BRAINLESS BUGS

A fire ant can survive without a brain because it has a network of nerves running down its back. These nerves **keep the ant in its zombie-like state,** and the maggot continues to feed and grow inside its body. After about two weeks, the maggot releases a chemical called an enzyme. This seeps into muscles in the back of the ant's head and dissolves them, **making the ant's head fall right off!** Following metamorphosis, the maggot transforms into the adult fly, which emerges from the dead ant.

SUPERHERO STYLE

POISON IVY
HER BODY PRODUCES MIND-CONTROLLING CHEMICAL PHEROMONES TO USE AGAINST ENEMIES.

PURPLE MAN
THIS SUPERVILLAIN RELEASES A CHEMICAL PHEROMONE INTO THE AIR. WHEN INHALED OR ABSORBED THROUGH THE SKIN, IT CAN BE USED FOR MIND CONTROL.

WOW!
THIS ANT HAS LOST ITS HEAD TO AN ANT-DECAPITATING FLY.

FEARSOME FAMILY

Belonging to a large family of phorid flies, ant-decapitating flies have some equally grisly relatives. Coffin flies are particularly gruesome, laying their eggs **on the remains of dead people.** The maggots continue to live inside their human hosts within the buried coffins, which give the flies their common name.

THE 'KISS OF DEATH' ASSASSIN BUG

Assassin bugs are a group of predatory insects that certainly live up to their common name. These small but deadly bugs strike with lightning speed to feast on the bodies and blood of animals such as bats, cattle and even people. They inject paralyzing venom into their prey, which then dissolves their victims' bodies from the inside out.

Belonging to a large group of around 4,000 different insect species, these predatory bugs live in many different parts of the world, from Africa and Europe to the Americas. **Assassin bugs are swift, fearless predators** that usually attack and eat other bugs – including members of their own species!

CRITTER STATS!

Size: 4-40 mm

Number of species: More than 4,000

Habitat: Worldwide, especially forests

THE HUMAN FACTOR

SOME ASSASSIN BUGS ARE HELPFUL TO GARDENERS AND FARMERS BECAUSE THEY PREY ON THE INSECT PESTS THAT DESTROY GARDEN PLANTS AND IMPORTANT CROPS.

SUPER NATURAL POWER!

Some assassin bugs have a more sinister side. They are known as 'kissing bugs' because they give people the 'kiss of death'. The bugs target soft parts of the body such as the lips. They use their sharp mouthparts to pierce through the soft skin and inject a chemical that paralyzes the flesh around the bite. The bugs are then free to feast on human blood.

DEADLY DISEASE

Some assassin bugs carry a tiny parasite, which enters the person's bloodstream when the bug bites. This parasite causes a deadly disease called Chagas disease, which is particularly common in Central and South America. In the early stages of the disease, the symptoms are often no more than a mild fever and swelling and pain around the bite. In many cases, these symptoms usually clear up within a few weeks. But people go on to develop permanent heart and digestive conditions, which can be deadly if left untreated.

AWESOME!

THESE BEASTLY BUGS OFTEN LIVE IN PEOPLE'S BEDS AND ATTACK AT NIGHT, WHEN PEOPLE ARE ASLEEP.

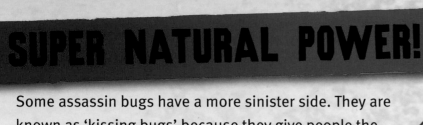

MEANWHILE, AT THE MOVIES...

SUPERHERO STYLE

COMIC-BOOK AND ACTION HEROES AND VILLAINS THAT POSSESS THE 'KISS OF DEATH' SUPERPOWER INCLUDE:

THE JOKER IN THE MOVIE 'THE DARK KNIGHT RETURNS', THE JOKER USES TOXIC LIPSTICK TO GIVE HIS OPPONENTS THE KISS OF DEATH.

ROGUE THIS X-MEN CHARACTER DISCOVERED HER 'KISS OF DEATH' SUPERPOWER WHEN SHE KISSED HER BOYFRIEND FOR THE FIRST TIME - AND PUT HIM INTO A COMA!

WOW!

AFTER PIERCING THE SKIN, AN ASSASSIN BUG PREPARES TO FEAST ON HUMAN BLOOD.

THE MURDEROUS WIDOW SPIDER

Widow spiders are a small group of venomous spiders that live in many different parts of the world, especially North America. It pays to be female if you are a widow spider. Females usually eat the males after mating with them!

There are four species within the group of widow spiders that take the name 'black widow spider'. Three are found in North America and one lives in central Asia and the Mediterranean region of Europe. Like all spiders, they have eight legs and a body divided into two parts – a head and a rear end called an abdomen – and **fang-bearing jaws called chelicerae.**

CRITTER STATS!

Size: Up to 40 mm long

Number of species: 31/32

Habitat: Most habitats around the world

WOW!

THE REDBACK SPIDER IS EASILY IDENTIFIED BY THE RED MARK ON THE BACK OF ITS ABDOMEN.

 **THE HUMAN FACTOR**

THE REDBACK SPIDER IS A WIDOW SPIDER THAT LIVES IN AUSTRALIA. ITS VENOM IS STRONG ENOUGH TO KILL AN ADULT PERSON – THOUGH CHILDREN AND OLDER ADULTS ARE MOST AT RISK. FORTUNATELY, SCIENTISTS HAVE DEVELOPED AN ANTIVENIN TO REDBACK BITES, SO THESE SPIDERS POSE LESS OF A THREAT THAN THEY ONCE DID. IN FACT, NO ONE HAS DIED FROM A REDBACK BITE SINCE THE ANTIVENIN WAS CREATED IN 1956.

SUPER NATURAL POWER!

Like all widow spiders, the black widow is as deadly to other widow spiders as it is to its prey. Female black widows commit the **ultimate crime of passion** – by eating the males after mating with them. Bizarrely enough, the male may encourage the female to commit her crime by **waving his colourful abdomen near her face** as they mate.

SPINNING SILK

The female – having built up her strength by feasting on her mate – lays around 300 eggs and **spins a cocoon of silk** around them. When the eggs hatch, the young spiders blow away in the wind. They build their first webs where they land.

Adult black widows build huge silk webs to trap prey such as insects and other bugs. The silk is also **strong enough to catch even bigger animals**, such as lizards. The spider then moves in and injects potent venom to paralyse and kill its prey.

SUPERHERO STYLE

NATALIA ROMANOVA
AN ATHLETIC SOVIET SUPERVILLAIN AND ENEMY OF IRON MAN, WHO LATER DEFECTED TO THE UNITED STATES AND JOINED THE AVENGERS SUPERHERO TEAM.

YELENA BELOVA
THE SECOND BLACK WIDOW, YELENA BELOVA WAS A SOVIET SPY AND ASSASSIN WHO ALSO HAD SUPERHUMAN ATHLETIC ABILITIES.

AWESOME!
WIDOW SPIDERS SPIN HUGE SILK WEBS AND COCOONS OF SILK IN THE SHAPE OF PING PONG BALLS.

THE EXPLOSIVE BOMBARDIER BEETLE

CRITTER STATS!

Size:
5 – 13 mm

Number of species:
Around 500

Habitat:
Woodlands and grassy places

These big, bulky beetles live in woodlands or grasslands around the world, with the exception of Antarctica. Most species, of which there are around 500, are ferocious carnivores, including the larvae, and the adults have a secret weapon to protect them from their main enemies – ants.

The bombardier beetle is the ultimate defender. This minibeast may not look like much, but it has a secret weapon – **it's packing heat.** Ants are the bombardier's arch-enemies. They swarm around the beetle, biting and nipping and trying to eat it. But the bombardier beetle has a seriously impressive superpower to help defend him. Well, actually, **it's up his bottom!**

THE HUMAN FACTOR

PEOPLE HAVE BEEN USING TOXIC CHEMICALS TO DEFEND THEMSELVES AND ATTACK THEIR ENEMIES FOR HUNDREDS OF YEARS. FROM MEDIEVAL SIEGES, DURING WHICH SOLDIERS TIPPED BOILING OIL AND INCENDIARY BOMBS ON ADVANCING SOLDIERS, TO MODERN-DAY CHEMICAL NERVE AGENTS, CHEMICAL WARFARE IS THE ULTIMATE DETERRENT ON THE BATTLEFIELD. CHEMICAL WEAPONS HAVE PROVED SO DEADLY THAT MOST COUNTRIES NOW AGREE THEY SHOULD NOT BE USED IN WAR.

Stored within the beetle's abdomen are two powerful liquids that the beetle can mix together, creating a chemical reaction that is so explosive that it sends **a jet of boiling, toxic acid** out of his rear all over attacking ants. The acid smells disgusting, and burns anything it touches. It's so hot that the beetle has to jet it out in pulses of **500 bursts per second** to stop him from burning his own bottom. The force of the explosion forces the liquid out of 'jets' in the beetle's body with a loud pop. The beetle can **swivel its bottom through 360 degrees** to direct the spray with amazing accuracy.

WOW!
THE ACID DISCHARGED BY A BOMBADIER BEETLE IS AS HOT AS BOILING WATER!

MEANWHILE, AT THE MOVIES...

SUPERHERO STYLE

COMIC-BOOK CHARACTERS AND ACTION HEROES WHO USE EXPLOSIVES TO PROTECT THEMSELVES INCLUDE:

NITRO
TURNS HIS BODY INTO A GAS AND EXPLODES WITH A FORCE EQUIVALENT TO HUNDREDS OF KILOGRAMMES OF DYNAMITE.

DAMAGE
RELEASES ENERGY IN THE FORM OF POWERFUL EXPLOSIONS. DAMAGE ACTUALLY STARTED ANOTHER BIG BANG EXPLOSION WHEN ONE OF HIS ENEMIES DESTROYED THE UNIVERSE.

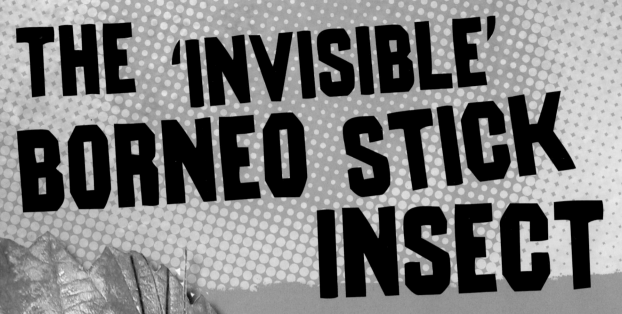

THE 'INVISIBLE' BORNEO STICK INSECT

The Borneo stick insect is the longest insect in the world. This slender bug can grow up to half a metre long and hides amongst the dense forest vegetation on an island called Borneo – part of a country called Indonesia. Borneo stick insects may be very long, but they are hard to spot thanks to their amazing camouflage.

Scientists found the longest Borneo stick insect in 2008 during an expedition to the rainforests of Borneo in Southeast Asia. When they measured it, they found it was 56.7 cm long – **about as long as your arm.** The scientists took the (dead) stick insect home to London, where it is on display at the Natural History Museum.

CRITTER STATS!

CRITTER STATS!

Size: Up to 57 cm long

Number of species: 1

Habitat: Dense vegetation

SUPER NATURAL POWER!

Like all stick insects, the Borneo stick insect is **a master of disguise**. It spends most of the day resting in the treetops. It has a long, thin, greenish-brown body and legs that look exactly like the branches of trees in which they live. To add to the camouflage, stick insects gently rock from side to side **just like branches swaying in the breeze**. At night, the Borneo stick insect becomes active and roams through the dense vegetation to feed on the plentiful supply of leaves.

MEANWHILE, AT THE MOVIES...

SUPERHERO STYLE

COMIC-BOOK CHARACTERS AND ACTION HEROES WHO CAN MIMIC THEIR ENEMIES OR USE CAMOUFLAGE INCLUDE:

AMAZO THIS DC COMICS CHARACTER CAN COPY THE ABILITIES AND SUPERPOWERS OF ANY SUPERHEROES HE MEETS.

NIGHTCRAWLER A MUTANT WITH SUPERHUMAN AGILITY, NIGHTCRAWLER USES CAMOUFLAGE TO BLEND INTO THE SHADOWS AND MOVE AROUND WITHOUT BEING SEEN.

LEAF-LIKE RELATIVES

Stick insects belong to a large group of about 3,000 species that also include leaf insects. These insects are **just as skilled at camouflage**, having green and brown bodies to match the colour of their leafy homes. Some species even have dark blotches and spots to copy the natural discolouration of real leaves.

AWESOME! AS THEIR NAME SUGGESTS, LEAF INSECTS LOOK EXACTLY LIKE THE LEAVES OF PLANTS.

DESERT LOCUST

MASS ATTACK!

Nothing strikes more fear into the hearts of hungry people than a plague of desert locusts. These six-legged supervillains usually live alone but may gather in gigantic swarms, devastating crops across millions of square kilometres. Desert locusts contribute to the problems of famine and starvation in developing countries, particularly in Africa, by eating the crops that people rely on for food.

The desert locust is one of about 15 species of locust. These large insects spend most of their time alone, living in the deserts of Africa, the Middle East and eastern parts of Asia. Unlike many insects, which undergo complete metamorphosis from an egg to a larva and then to the adult insect, locusts undergo incomplete metamorphosis. The young locusts, called nymphs, hatch as miniature versions of the adult insects and go through six stages of development. At each stage, the locust sheds its hard outer skin, called an exoskeleton, and grows into a new skin underneath.

CRITTER STATS!

Size: Up to 7.5 cm long
Number of species: 1
Habitat: Deserts of Africa, Asia and the Middle East

 **THE HUMAN FACTOR**

IN MANY COUNTRIES AROUND THE WORLD, PEOPLE RELY ON LOCUSTS AS A SOURCE OF FOOD. THE LOCUSTS ARE AN IMPORTANT SOURCE OF PROTEIN WHEN OTHER FOODS, PARTICULARLY PLANT CROPS, ARE IN SHORT SUPPLY – ALL THANKS TO THE HUNGRY LOCUST PESTS!

SUPER NATURAL POWER!

The solitary life of the desert locusts soon changes when it rains. This prompts the female to lay her eggs in the sandy desert soil. The rain spurs new plant growth, so there is food and shelter available for the nymphs when they hatch. **More and more locusts swarm around the plants,** which triggers changes in the insects' metabolism. First, they change colour and their bodies become shorter. Then **they release a chemical pheromone** that enhances the swarming behaviour.

PLAGUE PROPORTIONS

Very quickly, a swarm of locusts can **grow to epic proportions**. A single swarm can cover thousands of square kilometres, with **between 40 and 80 million locusts** in each square kilometre. The hungry swarm munches its way through any plants it meets – including important crops. **The last major plague occurred in 2004** in West Africa. Farmers in more than 20 countries lost up to US$2.5 billion worth of crops.

AWESOME!

A DESERT LOCUST CAN EAT ITS BODYWEIGHT IN PLANTS EVERY DAY, SO A SWARM OF HUNGRY LOCUSTS CAN HAVE DEVASTATING CONSEQUENCES ACROSS WIDE AREAS OF FARMLAND.

WOW!

A SWARM OF DESERT LOCUSTS CAN FLY UP TO 200 KILOMETRES EVERY DAY.

MEANWHILE, AT THE MOVIES...

SUPERHERO STYLE

MANY COMIC BOOK CHARACTERS JOIN FORCES TO FIGHT THEIR ENEMIES, WHILE ONE ANIMATED VILLAIN HAS EVEN APPEARED AS A GIANT LOCUST.

AVENGERS A CRACK TEAM OF MARVEL COMIC SUPERHEROES THAT ORIGINALLY INCLUDED IRON MAN, ANT-MAN, WASP, THOR AND HULK. CAPTAIN AMERICA JOINED THE AVENGERS AFTER THE TEAM FREED HIM FROM A BLOCK OF ICE.

ZORAK A GIANT LOCUST (OR PRAYING MANTIS, DEPENDING ON THE EPISODE) NAMED ZORAK APPEARED AS AN ADVERSARY TO SPACE GHOST IN THE 1990S CARTOON 'SPACE GHOST COAST TO COAST'.

THE SUPER-STRONG DUNG BEETLE

Can you imagine making your home in a pile of animal dung? One group of insects does exactly that – the aptly named dung beetles, which use their super sense of smell to home in on the nearest pile of animal droppings. This may seem gross, but these six-legged superheroes do a vital job, helping to clean the soil and recycle valuable nutrients.

There are many **thousands of different dung beetles** that live in most of the world's habitats, from deserts and farms to grasslands and forests. In fact, the only place where dung beetles cannot survive is in the frozen wasteland of Antarctica. These hardy beetles are so successful because they feed on a readily available food source that most other animals choose to ignore – **animal poo.**

CRITTER STATS!

Size: From 1mm to 6cm

Number of species: 30,000

Habitat: Most habitats

SUPERHERO STYLE

SEE THEM AT THE MOVIES!

WELL-KNOWN COMIC-BOOK CHARACTERS AND ACTION HEROES WITH BEETLE-LIKE SUPERPOWERS INCLUDE:

SCARAB THE SECRET IDENTITY OF EGYPTOLOGIST PETER WARD, WHO TRANSFORMED INTO A SUPER-POWERFUL SCARAB (DUNG) BEETLE WHEN HE RUBBED HIS MAGIC SCARAB RING. (THE ANCIENT EGYPTIANS WORSHIPPED DUNG BEETLES CALLED SCARABS.)

SILVER SCARAB ANOTHER BEETLE-BASED COMIC-BOOK CHARACTER WITH SUPERHUMAN STRENGTH AND THE ABILITY TO FLY IN OUTER SPACE.

SUPER NATURAL POWER!

Dung beetles use their **amazing sense of smell** to detect their next meal. Many species fly forwards and backwards across the wind until they pick up the scent of a pile of dung. Then they move upwind to locate their target.

Different dung beetles have different feeding strategies. Some **mould the animal dung into huge balls** and roll them around as a mobile food store. Others store animal droppings in underground 'larders'. A few species actually lay their eggs in the dung, and the larvae deplete the nutrients in the dung as they grow into adult beetles. **A freshly laid pile of dung** will attract numerous dung beetles in a matter of minutes.

AWESOME!

SCIENTISTS WORKING IN KRUGER NATIONAL PARK IN SOUTH AFRICA ONCE COUNTED 16,000 DUNG BEETLES IN A SINGLE PILE OF ELEPHANT POO!

WOW!

A SINGLE DUNG BEETLE CAN ROLL A BALL OF DUNG MANY TIMES ITS OWN WEIGHT.

BEETLE DRIVE

Along with their extrasensory scent detection, scientists think that dung beetles have an even more amazing superpower. In a recent study, scientists showed dung beetles might **use stars as a guide to help them roll balls of animal waste** along the ground. The study suggested that by following stars in the night sky, dung beetles roll their prized food source in a straight line away from the pile of animal dung, where other dung beetles might be waiting to steal it.

THE BIONIC EARTHWORM

CRITTER STATS!

Size: Up to 35 cm long
Number of species: 1
Habitat: Soil

The common earthworm is an invertebrate – an animal without a backbone. In fact, the earthworm is nothing more than a long segmented tube with a head at one end and a tail at the other. Earthworms burrow through the soil, feeding on dead and living plant and animal material buried in the ground. The most amazing thing about these simple creatures is their bionic ability to regenerate body segments.

The earthworm's body consists of ring-like segments covered with tiny hairs, which help the worm grip as they burrow under the ground. By squirming its body through the mud, **earthworms help to mix up and aerate the soil** and provide drainage channels for water running through the ground. **Earthworms are also natural recyclers.** They help clean up the soil by feeding on the rotting remains of plants and animals.

THE HUMAN FACTOR

EARTHWORMS ARE IMPORTANT TO PEOPLE FOR MANY DIFFERENT REASONS. NOT ONLY DO THEY MAINTAIN THE QUALITY OF THE SOIL, WE USE THEM IN A PRACTICE CALLED VERMICULTURE. THIS IS WHEN EARTHWORMS ARE USED IN COMPOST HEAPS TO DECOMPOSE HUMAN FOOD WASTE. IN SOME CULTURES, SUCH AS THE MAORI OF NEW ZEALAND, PEOPLE EAT EARTHWORMS – LOCALLY CALLED NOKE – AS A DELICACY. ANYONE FANCY WORM SPAGHETTI?

SUPER NATURAL POWER!

If you were cruel enough to cut a common earthworm in half, you might be surprised to find out that the head end develops into a new fully grown worm. **The bionic power of the earthworm** is a response to predators such as garden birds, moles, snakes and toads, which rely on the worms as an important food source. The first stage in this regeneration is the healing of the wound. Cells then start to grow beneath the wound, forming **a structure called a blastema**. Gradually, the mass of cells in the blastema lengthens and grows into a new tail end.

MEANWHILE, AT THE MOVIES...

SUPERHERO STYLE

COMIC-BOOK CHARACTERS AND ACTION HEROES AND VILLAINS WITH REGENERATIVE SUPERPOWERS INCLUDE:

THE DOCTOR
THE CENTRAL CHARACTER FROM THE POPULAR BBC TELEVISION SERIES 'DOCTOR WHO' CAN REGENERATE FROM BEING SEVERELY WOUNDED.

WOLVERINE
THIS MARVEL COMICS SUPERHERO HAS STAYED ALIVE DESPITE BEING SHOT MANY TIMES THANKS TO ENHANCED REGENERATIVE HEALING.

FEEDING FRENZY

Earthworms feed as they burrow through the soil. This forces mud through the earthworm's gut – a long, straight tube that runs from the mouth to the worm's bottom. The earthworm absorbs any food matter and the waste passes out through the worm's rear end and into the soil. You can see the earthworm's poo as worm casts on the surface of the soil.

AWESOME! CELLS GROW BENEATH THE HEAD END OF AN EARTHWORM'S BODY TO FORM A NEW TAIL END.

THE SUPER-STINGING FIRE ANT

There are more than 285 different fire ant species that live in most places around the world. These small insects have many different common names, including ginger ants, red ants and tropical red ants. Fire ants inject venom using a stinger instead of spraying acid over attackers like many other ant species.

Fire ants are typical insects, with three distinct body segments – the head, thorax and abdomen – a pair of antennae on the head and three pairs of legs on each body segment. **These ants live in large groups called colonies.** They build nests in the soil, which are usually hidden underneath logs or rocks. In open spaces, the ants often build their nest and cover it with a large mound of soil.

SUPER NATURAL POWER!

Most ants attack their enemies by biting them and then **spraying a corrosive chemical** called formic acid over the bite wound. Fire ants also bite but only to grasp on to their opponent. Once it has got a good grip, **the ant then injects venom** using a stinger in its tail. The venom is potent enough to kill most prey animals and is an effective weapon against most predators.

When people are stung by fire ants they experience a **strong burning sensation.** In most cases, the area of the sting swells into a bump for a few days and then disappears. In a few serious cases, people can have an allergic reaction to the sting, which can be **fatal without emergency treatment.**

ANT JOBS

Different ants have different roles within the colony. All colonies contain at least one queen ant. The queen pairs up with male ants called drones, which die immediately after mating. The queen then lays her eggs – **up to 3,500 eggs every day**. The soldier ants guard all the other ants in the colony. They have bigger jaws, called mandibles, to bite their enemies. The workers do all the other jobs in the colony, such as cleaning, foraging for food and caring for the larvae.

AWESOME!
A FIRE ANT PREPARES TO ATTACK ITS HUMAN VICTIM WITH ITS EXTREMEMLY PAINFUL STING.

SUPERHERO STYLE

MISS ARROW THIS MARVEL VILLAIN DELIVERS HER POTENT VENOM USING STINGERS THAT GENERATE FROM HER WRISTS.

THE JOKER BATMAN'S ARCH-ENEMY SOMETIMES USES A TOXIC CHEMICAL COCKTAIL CALLED JOKER VENOM TO IMMOBILIZE HIS OPPONENTS.

WOW!
QUEEN ANTS ARE THE BIGGEST AND MOST IMPORTANT MEMBERS OF A FIRE ANT COLONY.

THE HIGH-JUMPING BLOOD-SUCKING FLEA

CRITTER STATS!

Size: Up to 3.5 mm

Number of species: 2000

Habitat: Parasitic

Fleas are wingless insects that live on the bodies of host animals such as birds and mammals. These small parasites have sharp piercing mouthparts to break through the skin of their hosts and drink up their blood. One of the flea's most amazing superpowers is its ability to jump great distances.

There are more than 2,000 different flea species that live on the bodies of a number of different **warm-blooded hosts**, from cats and chickens to rats, dogs and even people.

THE HUMAN FACTOR

IN MEDIEVAL EUROPE, FLEAS LIVING ON RATS SPREAD ONE OF THE DEADLIEST DISEASES IN HUMAN HISTORY – BUBONIC PLAGUE, ALSO KNOWN AS THE BLACK DEATH. FLEAS ARE RESPONSIBLE FOR SPREADING MANY OTHER HUMAN DISEASES, INCLUDING CAT-SCRATCH DISEASE AND TAPEWORM INFECTIONS.

WOW!
THE RED MARK ON THE CAT'S SKIN SHOWS THAT IT HAS BEEN BITTEN BY A FLEA.

SUPER NATURAL POWER!

Most fleas are small insects, measuring no more than 3.5 mm in length. But they can jump up to 18 cm directly upwards and more than 30 cm across – from a standstill!

The amazing jumping ability of the flea is not due to muscle power. Instead, these insects use the energy stored in a protein called resilin, which is found in the flea's long back legs. This substance provides the spring action to get the flea airborne. The flea then homes in on the body heat and vibrations of its host.

FANTASTIC FLEAS

Fleas have a number of adaptations to life as parasitic insects. For a start, they have flattened bodies, which means they can move easily through the fur or feathers that cover the bodies of their hosts. The flea's body is also hard, shiny and **covered with backward-pointing hairs** and spines, which also help the fleas move about on their hosts. The body of the flea is also tough – **it is almost impossible to squash a flea** with your fingers. This is probably another adaptation to life as a parasite, preventing the host from **scratching or crushing the flea to kill it.**

AWESOME!
THE FLEA IS ONE OF THE BEST JUMPERS OF THE ANIMAL KINGDOM, RELATIVE TO ITS BODY SIZE. IT IS SHOWN HERE AS SEEN UNDER AN ELECTRON MICROSCOPE.

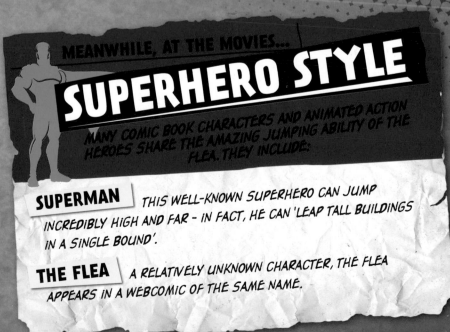

MEANWHILE, AT THE MOVIES...

SUPERHERO STYLE

MANY COMIC BOOK CHARACTERS AND ANIMATED ACTION HEROES SHARE THE AMAZING JUMPING ABILITY OF THE FLEA. THEY INCLUDE:

SUPERMAN THIS WELL-KNOWN SUPERHERO CAN JUMP INCREDIBLY HIGH AND FAR – IN FACT, HE CAN 'LEAP TALL BUILDINGS IN A SINGLE BOUND'.

THE FLEA A RELATIVELY UNKNOWN CHARACTER, THE FLEA APPEARS IN A WEBCOMIC OF THE SAME NAME.

THE FUNGUS GNAT

GLOW WORM

These glow worms are the larvae of one of four species of fungus gnats – tiny, short-lived flies that live in caves and sheltered forests of Australia and New Zealand. The tiny flies belong to the group (genus) Arachnocampa, which means 'spider worm'.

Fungus gnats spend most of their lives as larvae. After mating with the male, the female fungus gnat lays her eggs in two or three clumps of 40 to 50 eggs. The larvae hatch about 20 days later, and they spin a silk nest on a cave roof or overhanging branch. The larvae then spin up to 70 silky threads and hang them from the bottom of the nest. Each thread holds **sticky blobs of mucus to snare passing prey** – anything from caddis flies and mayflies to moths and mosquitoes. The sticky mucus blobs contain venom to **paralyse and subdue the prey** to make it easier to eat.

WOW!

THE GLOW WORMS MIMIC SPIDERS BY HANGING STICKY SILK THREADS FROM THE ROOF OF A CAVE, USING THEM TO CATCH PREY.

CRITTER STATS!

Size: Up to 3 cm
Number of species: 4
Habitat: Caves and sheltered forests

SUPER NATURAL POWER!

The fungus gnat larva is often called a glow worm because it glows in the dark. Since the female lays her eggs in clumps, there can be hundreds of glowing larvae on the cave roof, and they look like stars in the sky at night. This glowing light show lures prey towards the sticky threads below the nests. When a fly or other unfortunate victim hits the sticky snare, it becomes trapped. The larva then slowly pulls the victim up on its thread to feed.

LETHAL LIGHT LURE

An amazing process called bioluminescence gives the fungus gnat its glow. The larva produces a chemical called luciferin, which is stored in the gnat larva's abdomen. This substance reacts with an enzyme and oxygen to glow brightly. The glow dims after the larvae have eaten, so the hungriest larvae glow the brightest.

AWESOME!

THE GLOWING LIGHT SHOW LURES PREY TOWARDS THE STICKY THREADS BELOW THE NESTS.

LIFE CYCLE

The fungus gnats live as larvae for up to 12 months. Then, they pupate, which means they form a cocoon and transform into the adult gnats. The females continue to glow, which attracts the males to mate with them. After mating, the female lays her eggs and the life cycle continues.

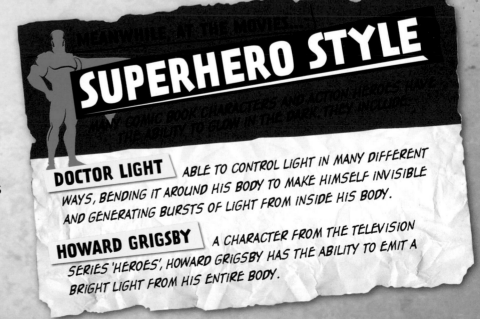

MEANWHILE, AT THE MOVIES...

SUPERHERO STYLE

MANY COMIC BOOK CHARACTERS AND ACTION HEROES HAVE THE ABILITY TO GLOW IN THE DARK. THEY INCLUDE:

DOCTOR LIGHT ABLE TO CONTROL LIGHT IN MANY DIFFERENT WAYS, BENDING IT AROUND HIS BODY TO MAKE HIMSELF INVISIBLE AND GENERATING BURSTS OF LIGHT FROM INSIDE HIS BODY.

HOWARD GRIGSBY A CHARACTER FROM THE TELEVISION SERIES 'HEROES', HOWARD GRIGSBY HAS THE ABILITY TO EMIT A BRIGHT LIGHT FROM HIS ENTIRE BODY.

THE GIANT GOLIATH
BIRD-EATING SPIDER

The goliath bird-eating spider is a monster-sized tarantula with a huge appetite to match its gigantic size. This deadly arachnid takes its name from the eyewitness reports of 19th century English explorers, who saw them feasting on hummingbirds in the rainforests of South America.

One of the world's biggest arachnids, no other spider comes near to matching the goliath bird-eating spider's huge body mass. Only one other species – the giant huntsman spider – has a bigger leg span.

Although the goliath bird-eating spider is definitely big enough to eat a bird, this hardly ever happens. These spiders live underground in burrows and seldom chance upon bird prey other than chicks that have fallen out of their nests near the entrance to their burrows.

WOW!

THE SHARP FANGS AND HAIRY BODY OF THE GOLIATH BIRD-EATING SPIDER MAKE IT A FORMIDABLE FOE.

CRITTER STATS!

Size: Leg span of 30cm
Number of species: 1
Habitat: South American rainforests

SUPER NATURAL POWER!

The goliath bird-eating spider is armed with a deadly arsenal. The spider's fangs (see right) are as long and as sharp as a cat's claws and can **puncture through flesh with ease**. These spiders are ambush predators and sit at the entrance to their burrows, waiting for passing prey. When a suitably sized animal passes by, the spider darts forward and **injects venom into the body of its victim**. The venom paralyses the helpless prey, leaving the spider free to feed.

HAIR RAISING!

Despite its long, sharp fangs, the goliath bird-eating spider will only bite as a last resort. The body of **this spider is extraordinarily hairy** and provides the arachnid with a clever form of defence. When threatened, most spiders will simply retreat to the safety of their burrows and wait for the danger to pass. But the goliath bird-eating spider also uses its legs to kick hairs on its abdomen towards an attacker. The goliath bird-eating spider rubs its legs together, **creating a hissing sound** to ward off unwanted attention. The hairs are covered with tiny spines and are irritating if they come into contact with the skin, eyes or mouth.

MEANWHILE, AT THE MOVIES...

SUPERHERO STYLE

WELL-KNOWN COMIC BOOK CHARACTERS AND ACTION HEROES WITH SIMILAR SPIDER-LIKE WEAPONRY INCLUDE:

SPIDER-MAN THE ALTER-EGO OF PETER PARKER, WHO WAS BITTEN BY A RADIOACTIVE SPIDER WHEN HE WAS A TEENAGER, WHICH GAVE HIM HIS AMAZING ARACHNID POWERS.

BLACK WIDOW THE ARCH-ENEMY OF IRON MAN, WHO LATER PUT HER AMAZING SPIDER-LIKE AGILITY TO GOOD USE IN THE FIGHT AGAINST EVIL SUPERPOWERS.

AWESOME!
AS NOCTURNAL CREATURES THESE SPIDERS ARE ACTIVE AT NIGHT, SPENDING THE DAY IN DAMP, DARK BURROWS.

THE SUPER-STRONG HERCULES BEETLE

The Hercules beetle is one of six species of rhinoceros beetles, which live in the tropical rainforests of Central and South America. Named after the super-strong hero of Greek legend, the Hercules beetle is, for its size, one of the world's strongest animals.

The biggest of the six rhinoceros beetles, the Hercules beetle is **one of the largest beetles in the world.** Only the colossal titan beetle, which also lives in the rainforests of South America, is bigger. The long 'rhino' horns of the Hercules beetle make up most of its length. Only male beetles have the giant horns. The female beetles have bigger bodies but, without the long horns, are always shorter than the males.

CRITTER STATS!

Size: Up to 17 cm
Number of species: 1
Habitat: Tropical rainforests

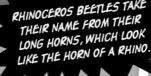

RHINOCEROS BEETLES TAKE THEIR NAME FROM THEIR LONG HORNS, WHICH LOOK LIKE THE HORN OF A RHINO.

SUPER NATURAL POWER!

The Hercules beetle takes its common name from the Greek hero Hercules, who was noted for his amazing strength and fearless nature. The Hercules beetle certainly lives up to its name. While a single beetle weighs in at about 85g, it can lift **up to 850 times its own body weight** – that's the same as an adult human lifting ten African elephants!

FANCY THAT!

The horns of the male beetles may look like formidable weapons, but they are rarely used for this purpose. In fact, male beetles use their long horns to **show off their strength and fitness** to the females. Males with longer horns will usually attract more females. On rare occasions, two males will fight for the affection of the female. The winner is the male that **flips his rival onto his back**.

FEMALE HERCULES BEETLES HAVE LARGER BODIES THAN THE MALES.

MEANWHILE AT THE MOVIES...

SUPERHERO STYLE

SEVERAL COMIC BOOK CHARACTERS AND ACTION HEROES ARE NOTED FOR THEIR AMAZING STRENGTH. THEY INCLUDE:

SUPERMAN

THIS FAMOUS SUPERHERO IS THE MOST POWERFUL OF ALL LIVING THINGS AND HAS SHOWN SEVERAL SUPERHUMAN FEATS OF STRENGTH. SUPERMAN CAN LIFT MORE THAN ONE MILLION TONNES WITH EASE.

THE INCREDIBLE HULK

ONE OF THE STRONGEST SUPERHEROES OF ALL, HULK GETS EVEN STRONGER THE ANGRIER HE BECOMES.

AWESOME!

DESPITE THEIR FEARSOME APPEARANCE, HERCULES BEETLES ARE HERBIVORES, FEEDING ON RIPE AND DECAYING FRUIT.

THE HIMALAYAN 'HIGH' JUMPING

SPIDER

The Himalayan jumping spider is a tiny acrobatic arachnid that literally lives on top of the world – high on the slopes of the world's tallest mountain, Mount Everest. In fact, this hardy jumping spider manages to survive at more than 6,700 metres above sea level, making it one of the highest-known living animals on Earth!

The scientific species name of the Himalayan jumping spider is *omnisuperstes*, which means 'standing above everything'. These brave spiders are certainly one of the few animals that can survive at such a high altitude. They brave the **wild winds and freezing mountain temperatures** by hiding in rock crevices.

CRITTER STATS!

Size: Around 15 mm
Number of species: 1
Habitat: High mountains

THE HIMALAYAN JUMPING SPIDER LIVES ON TOP OF THE WORLD, ON THE SLOPES OF MOUNT EVEREST.

SUPER NATURAL POWER!

Since there are no other living animals that make their home high in mountains, Himalayan jumping spiders feed on stray insects and other debris that blow up from the lower slopes. Like all jumping spiders, this high-altitude arachnid does not spin a web to trap passing insects. Instead, it spins a single silk thread and **uses it as a safety cord** to anchor its body to a rock or other solid object.

MEANWHILE, AT THE MOVIES...

SUPERHERO STYLE

COMIC BOOK CHARACTERS AND ACTION HEROES WHO DEMONSTRATE AN AMAZING JUMPING ABILITY INCLUDE:

SPIDER-MAN

SPIDER-MAN IS FAMOUS FOR HIS SUPERHUMAN LEAPING SKILLS AND CAN LEAP BETWEEN BUILDINGS WITH EASE, USING WEBLINES TO HELP HIM.

SUPERMAN

SUPERMAN WAS ONE OF THE FIRST SUPERHEROES TO USE ENHANCED JUMPING AND WAS 'ABLE TO LEAP TALL BUILDINGS IN A SINGLE BOUND'.

SPRING ACTION

When an insect floats past in the wind, **the spider springs into action**. It uses a rapid pulse of hydraulic pressure in its back legs to pounce on passing insects. In this way, **the jumping spider can leap incredible distances** – many times its own body size. If the spider misses its prey, it simply pulls itself back along the safety cord (seen at the top right of this picture) and waits for another opportunity to feed.

SAFETY CORD

AWESOME!

THERE ARE MORE THAN 5,000 SPECIES OF JUMPING SPIDER. THEY ALL HUNT FOR PREY USING THEIR FANTASTIC EYESIGHT AND AMAZING JUMPING ABILITY.

THE ANTI-GRAVITY SUPER-SENSORY HOUSEFLY

The common housefly is the fly you will most often find flying around inside your home, buzzing around and generally causing a nuisance. These pesky pests have such a bad reputation because they spread so many diseases. Houseflies have an amazing array of supernatural senses and can even defy gravity by walking upside down!

Houseflies spend a lot of time crawling over **animal poo, rubbish and rotting flesh.** After these pests feed and lay their eggs on this putrid mess, they fly into our homes and spread the germs all over our food and belongings. Yuk! These are the same germs that cause a number of **potentially deadly diseases,** including cholera, tuberculosis and typhoid fever.

CRITTER STATS!

Size: 2 cm long
Number of species: 1
Habitat: Worldwide

THE HUMAN FACTOR

HOUSEFLIES MAY HAVE A NUMBER OF DISGUSTING HABITS, BUT THEY ARE ALSO HELPFUL TO PEOPLE AND OTHER ANIMALS. FIRST, HOUSEFLIES AND THEIR LARVAE ALSO PROVIDE FOOD FOR MANY DIFFERENT CREATURES. THE FLIES ALSO HELP RECYCLE NUTRIENTS AND CLEAN UP THE ENVIRONMENT BY BREAKING DOWN WASTE MATERIAL.

SUPER NATURAL POWER!

If you have ever tried to swat a housefly, you will know how frustrating it can be. They seem to second-guess every swipe and you end up missing more times than scoring a hit. **Houseflies have an array of sharp senses** – primarily to avoid the many predators that want to eat them. First, houseflies have excellent all-round vision, with two large compound eyes containing 6,000 individual lenses each. They also have three extra simple eyes, which act like a compass and tell the fly which way is up.

FANTASTIC FEET

Houseflies also have fantastic senses of smell and taste. They smell using their antennae and taste with their long tongue, called a proboscis. In addition, houseflies can taste food with their feet! These super-sensitive feet also provide the housefly with its **amazing anti-gravity crawling abilities**. Each footpad has tiny claws and moist suction cups called pulvilli, which allow the fly to grip onto slippery glass surfaces and even crawl upside down.

FEEDING FRENZY

If you think the housefly's choice of food is gross, then you will definitely not like its table manners! The housefly cannot bite or chew so they cannot eat solid food. Instead, it vomits a mixture of saliva and digestive juices over its meal before sucking up the liquid goo.

WOW!
A HOUSEFLY'S FEET ARE TEN MILLION TIMES MORE SENSITIVE THAN THE HUMAN TONGUE.

MEANWHILE, AT THE MOVIES...

SUPERHERO STYLE

COMIC BOOK CHARACTERS AND ACTION HEROES WITH AN AWESOME ANTI-GRAVITY CLIMBING ABILITY INCLUDE:

NIGHTCRAWLER THIS SUPERHERO CAN SCALE SHEER SURFACES WITH EASE USING SUCTION CUPS ATTACHED TO HIS HANDS AND FEET.

SPIDER-MAN SPIDER-MAN IS ONE OF THE MOST FAMOUS SUPERHEROES WHO USES HIS WALL-CRAWLING ABILITY TO STICK TO SEEMINGLY IMPOSSIBLE SURFACES SUCH AS GLASS.

THE BOILING JAPANESE HONEYBEE

The Japanese honeybee is the Asian relative of the European honeybee. These insects range over much of southern and Southeast Asia, where they nest in enclosed spaces such as hollow tree trunks. Japanese honeybees will do almost anything to protect the hive – including cooking its enemies alive!

Japanese honeybees are social insects that live in groups called colonies. **A colony may contain up to 40,000 bees**. Every bee has a specific job, from the egg-laying queen to the industrious workers. The queen uses **chemicals called pheromones** to signal to other members of the colony. This tells the workers that she is fertile. The workers communicate to each other using complex 'dances'. In this way, they communicate the location of nearby sources of food (plant nectar) and water.

SUPER NATURAL POWER!

The Asian giant hornet (right) is the main predator of the Japanese honeybee. The hornets are deadly killers – 30 to 40 can wipe out an entire colony of bees in a few hours, using their massive mandibles (jaws) to **tear the bees and their larvae apart**. However, the bees sometimes fight back...

The hornets usually send out a scout to search for honeybee hives. When it does, the hornet scout crawls inside and **sprays the bees with a pheromone**. This acts as a signal to other hornets to home in on the hive. But the hornet is in for a nasty surprise. Hundreds of bees soon swarm around the hornet scout and start to rub their wings together. This raises the temperature inside the hive to 47°C (117°F), and **the hornet is slowly cooked alive.**

MEANWHILE, AT THE MOVIES...

SUPERHERO STYLE

SEVERAL COMIC BOOK CHARACTERS AND ACTION HEROES HARNESS THE POWER OF HEAT AS A SUPERPOWER. THEY INCLUDE:

HUMAN TORCH THIS FIERY SUPERHERO HAS THE ABILITY TO ENVELOP HIS BODY WITH SUPERHOT PLASMA AND SHOOT FIREBALLS AT HIS ENEMIES.

MAGMA THIS FEMALE SUPERHERO HARNESSES THE NATURAL HEAT FROM EARTH'S CORE TO FIGHT HER RIVALS.

WOW!
A HEATED MOUND OF HONEYBEES SWAMPS ITS WOULD-BE ATTACKERS...

AWESOME!
THE SWARM DEPARTS, LEAVING THE BODIES OF THE DEAD HORNETS BEHIND.

THE DEADLY MOSQUITO

Mosquitoes live in most parts of the world, except Antarctica. These tiny flies may look harmless, but they are one of the most dangerous animals on Earth. Female mosquitoes are pests with a thirst for blood. When they feed on human blood, some species pass on parasites that cause the deadly disease malaria.

There are more than 3,000 different mosquito species, but only a few carry the parasites that spread malaria. These mosquitoes live in tropical parts of the world, including Africa, Asia and Central and South America. Mosquitoes are **equipped with a range of super-senses** to home in on their next meal.

CRITTER STATS!

Size: Up to 16 mm
Number of species: More than 3,000
Habitat: Worldwide

THE HUMAN FACTOR

MALARIA IS THE ONE OF THE WORLD'S DEADLIEST DISEASES. EVERY YEAR, HUNDREDS OF MILLIONS OF PEOPLE ARE INFECTED WITH MALARIA PARASITES, AND MILLIONS MORE DIE. ONE OF THE BEST WAYS TO STOP THE SPREAD OF MALARIA IS BY SLEEPING UNDER A MOSQUITO NET.

AWESOME!

MOSQUITOES USE THEIR LARGE COMPOUND EYES TO TRACK THE MOVEMENTS OF THEIR PREY.

SUPER NATURAL POWER!

Mosquitoes rely on **chemical, visual and thermal clues** to sense their prey. The mosquito's antennae are sensitive to chemicals such as carbon monoxide and lactic acid, which are produced as by-products of our normal breathing. Mosquitoes also have excellent eyesight and see in colour, so they can easily spot a tourist in bright shorts and a tee shirt!

Chemicals in our sweat also attract mosquitoes, and sweating is hard to avoid in hot, tropical countries. In addition, mosquitoes home in on the body heat of their prey – so warm-blooded humans are fairly easy for mosquitoes to find.

PASSING ON PARASITES

Female mosquitoes pass on the parasites that cause malaria when they feed on human blood. They use their long proboscis to penetrate the skin and reach into the blood vessels below. To prevent the blood from clotting, the mosquitoes **inject saliva into the wound**. This saliva contains the malaria parasites, which then pass into the bloodstream and cause the disease.

WOW!
A MOSQUITO USES ITS LONG PROBOSCIS TO PIERCE HUMAN SKIN.

MEANWHILE, AT THE MOVIES...

SUPERHERO STYLE

COMIC-BOOK CHARACTERS AND SUPERHEROES WHO RELY ON BLOOD TO GIVE THEM SUPERNATURAL POWERS INCLUDE:

BLADE   THIS MARVEL COMICS SUPERHERO HAS MANY SUPERHUMAN ABILITIES, SUCH AS STRENGTH, STAMINA, SPEED AND AGILITY – AS WELL AS AN INSATIABLE APPETITE FOR BLOOD!

DRACULA   PERHAPS THE WORLD'S MOST FAMOUS VAMPIRE, COUNT DRACULA IS THE CENTRAL CHARACTER IN THE GOTHIC HORROR NOVEL BY IRISH WRITER BRAM STOKER.

AWESOME!
ITS BODY RED WITH BLOOD, A MOSQUITO FEEDS ON ITS HUMAN PREY.

THE ARMOURED MOTH BUTTERFLY CATERPILLAR

The caterpillar of the moth butterfly *Liphyra brassolis* lives in the tropical rainforests of southern and Southeast Asia and Australia. The moth butterfly is fairly unremarkable as an adult, but the caterpillar has built a reputation as a bit of brute! This carnivorous caterpillar has an unusual appetite for weaver ants.

The female moth butterfly lays her eggs on the underside of branches, carefully selecting trees that are home to colonies of weaver ants. The ants live in nests built from leaves, which are held together using **sticky strands of silk**. One tree may contain several ant nests, and each nest may be home to hundreds of worker ants, a queen, and the ant grubs. After about three weeks, the moth butterfly egg hatches. The caterpillar then makes its home in an ant nest, **attacking and feasting on the hundreds of larvae inside.**

AWESOME!

WEAVER ANTS WORK TOGETHER TO BUILD A NEST, BUT WILL IT BE UNDER THREAT FROM THE MOTH BUTTERFLY CATERPILLAR?

CRITTER STATS!

Size: About 3 cm
Number of species: 1
Habitat: Rainforests

SUPER NATURAL POWER!

Ants are not the most welcome of hosts – they bite and consume most intruders – **but the moth butterfly caterpillar thrives inside the nest**. These gatecrashers survive because they have thick, tough skin – the ants cannot bite through this **heavy suit of armour**. The ants even try to flip the caterpillar onto its back to attack the softer underside, but the caterpillar has strong, sucker-like feet to stick it firmly in place.

ANT ATTACK!

So the helpless ants can only watch in horror as the moth butterfly caterpillar starts to attack the ant grubs. The caterpillar drags them under its protective shield, sucks out the juices and discards the empty shell before moving on to its next victim. A hungry caterpillar can **devour as many as ten grubs every hour**.

WOW!
WITH ITS TOUGH SKIN AND SUCKER-LIKE FEET, THIS CATERPILLAR CAN REPEL ANY ANT-ATTACK.

MEANWHILE, AT THE MOVIES...

SUPERHERO STYLE

COMIC BOOK CHARACTERS AND ACTION HEROES AND VILLAINS WHO USE DEFENSIVE BODY ARMOUR INCLUDE:

IRON MAN WEARS A POWERED SUIT OF ARMOUR THAT GIVES HIM SUPERHUMAN STRENGTH AND AGILITY, AS WELL AS THE ABILITY TO FLY.

THE THING THE BODY OF THIS MARVEL SUPERHERO IS COVERED WITH AN ORANGE, FLEXIBLE, ROCK-LIKE HIDE, WHICH PROTECTS HIM FROM BULLETS, BOMBS AND OTHER WEAPONS.

AWESOME!
FUELLED BY ANT LARVAE, THIS CATERPILLAR HAS BEGUN ITS TRANSFORMATION INTO A MOTH BUTTERFLY.

THE TRANSPARENT SNAIL

The transparent snail is a miniature mollusc that lives in central and Western Europe, creeping across alpine meadows and woodlands in search of plant food. The most amazing thing about these tiny snails is their see-through shells, which give them an air of invisibility.

Like most land snails, the transparent snail has a **huge appetite for plants**. It eats the flowers, fruits, leaves and succulent tree bark, as well as the rotting remains of plant parts. Snails have a hard, rough structure called a radula inside their mouths. The radula is like a bit like a nail file, with **rows of tiny teeth** that scrape and grind up plant food. Occasionally, the transparent snail will eat dead earthworms and horse manure.

WOW!

DUE TO THEIR APPEARANCE, TRANSPARENT SNAILS ARE OFTEN ALSO KNOWN AS GLASS SNAILS.

CRITTER STATS!

Size: Up to 6 mm
Number of species: 1
Habitat: Moist, shady places

SUPER NATURAL POWER!

Most snails are born with soft, transparent shells. As they develop into adults, the shells usually harden and form their final colour (like the snail in the picture at the top of this page). But the **paper-thin shell** of the transparent snail (see below) stays see-through for its whole life, giving the snail a **ghostly, invisible appearance.**

THE HUMAN FACTOR

SNAILS ARE THE NUMBER ONE ENEMY OF FARMERS AND GARDENERS. THESE PESKY PESTS CAUSE A LOT OF DAMAGE IN GARDENS AND FARMS BECAUSE THEY RUIN IMPORTANT CROPS AND DECORATIVE GARDEN PLANTS AS THEY FEED.

SLEEPING SNAILS

Snails hibernate in the cold winter, burying in the soil and falling asleep for months. Before they hibernate, the snail seals up the entrance to its shell with a thick layer of slime, which then hardens into a tough skin. The skin protects the snail from **predators such as hedgehogs**. Air passes through a tiny hole in the skin so the snail can breathe when it is hibernating.

MEANWHILE, AT THE MOVIES...

SUPERHERO STYLE

COMIC-BOOK CHARACTERS AND ACTION HEROES WHO USE INVISIBILITY AS A SUPERPOWER INCLUDE:

INVISIBLE WOMAN

ASSUMED THE POWER OF INVISIBILITY AFTER BEING EXPOSED TO A COSMIC STORM. INVISIBLE WOMAN CAN RENDER HERSELF AND ANYONE SHE TOUCHES WHOLLY OR PARTIALLY INVISIBLE AT WILL.

PREDATOR

AN ALIEN FROM THE 1987 MOVIE OF THE SAME NAME, PREDATOR LOSES ITS INVISIBILITY POWER WHEN SUBMERGED IN WATER.

THE CRYOGENIC WOOLLY BEAR CATERPILLAR

The woolly bear caterpillar is the common name given to the larva of the Isabella Tiger Moth. These moths are found throughout North America, including the bitterly cold northern part of the continent. The hardy caterpillars hibernate during the harsh Arctic winter and literally freeze solid to survive.

The woolly bear caterpillar takes its name from the **thick dense bristles, called setae,** which cover its plump body. These setae give the caterpillar a furry appearance. In fact, they help the caterpillar move by gripping the surface of the ground. Unlike many caterpillar species, the setae of the woolly bear caterpillar do not inject venom, although they may irritate your skin if you pick one up.

SUPER NATURAL POWER!

Woolly bear caterpillars hatch from eggs in the late autumn and feed constantly to bulk up their bodies. As winter approaches, the temperature drops to well below freezing. The woolly bear caterpillar stops eating, its heart slows to a standstill and the blood, guts and rest of its body **freeze solid**.

MEANWHILE, AT THE MOVIES...

SUPERHERO STYLE

COMIC BOOK CHARACTERS AND ACTION HEROES AND VILLAINS WITH CRYOGENIC SUPERPOWERS INCLUDE

FROZONE

APPEARS IN THE 2004 MOVIE THE INCREDIBLES. FROZONE IS A LONG-TIME FRIEND OF MR. INCREDIBLE AND HAS THE POWER TO FREEZE WATER AT WILL, TRAVELLING AROUND ON CHUTES OF ICE.

MR FREEZE

THIS VILLAIN WEARS A CRYOGENIC SUIT TO SURVIVE AND PLANS HIS CRIMES AROUND THE THEMES OF ICE AND COLD. MR FREEZE IS ONE OF BATMAN'S ARCH-ENEMIES.

CHEMICAL PROTECTION

Most animals would literally freeze to death, but a chemical called a cryoprotectant **protects the caterpillar in its frozen state**. In the spring, when the temperatures rise, the caterpillar gently thaws out and its **heart starts beating again**. The caterpillar is then ready to pupate, wrapping a silk cocoon around its body and transforming into the adult Isabella Tiger moth (right).

WOW!
THE LIFE CYCLE OF THE ISABELLA TIGER MOTH TAKES 14 YEARS FROM EGG TO ADULT.

AWESOME!
THE CATERPILLARS WILL SPEND JUST FIVE PER CENT OF THEIR LIVES FEEDING AND UP TO 90 PER CENT IN THEIR FROZEN STATE.

GLOSSARY

abdomen The end part of an insect's body, after the head and thorax.

antivenin A chemical that is used to treat venomous bites and stings.

bioluminescence The ability of some living things to emit light and glow in the dark.

camouflage A tactic animals use (by changing colour or shape) to blend in with their surroundings.

carnivore An animal that only eats meat.

cocoon A silky case spun by the larvae of many insects to protect them as they transform into adult insects.

colony A group of animals that live together.

cryoprotectant A chemical that prevents the bodies of living things from freezing to death.

enzyme A chemical that speeds up chemical reactions that take place in the bodies of living things.

exoskeleton The hard outer skin of an insect or other animal.

fang The hollow tooth of an animal, such as a spider. The spider uses its fangs to inject venom into prey.

habitat The natural home of an animal.

hibernate To spend the winter months in a dormant or resting state.

invertebrate An animal without a backbone.

larva The young form of bugs that undergo complete metamorphosis.

mandibles The jaws and mouthparts of insects and other bugs.

metabolism The chemical processes that take place inside the body of an animal.

metamorphosis The gradual process of change from a young form of an animal into its adult form (such as a tadpole into a frog).

mollusc An invertebrate with a soft, unsegmented body that is usually contained within a hard shell.

nymph The young form of some invertebrates, particularly insects.

ovipositor The long tube female insects use to deposit their eggs.

parasite An organism that lives on another organism and benefits at the host's expense.

pheromone A chemical released by some living things to signal to members of the same species.

predator An animal that hunts and eats other animals.

prey An animal that is hunted and eaten by other animals.

proboscis The long sucking mouthparts of some bugs.

species A group of living things that can reproduce.

thorax The middle part of an insect's body between the head and the abdomen.

venom A poisonous secretion of an animal such as a snake, which is usually delivered by a bite.

FURTHER INFORMATION

BOOKS TO READ

Extraordinary Bugs. Leon Gray, Wayland, 2011.
Deadly Factbook: Insects and Spiders, Steve Backshall,
Orion Children's Books, 2012.
Incredible Insects. Jen Green, Armadillo Books, 2013.

WEBSITES TO VISIT

http://iloveinsects.wordpress.com
The weblog of entomology student Erika Lenz, this site is devoted to all things
insects and spiders – with some great video links, images and careers advice
for students interested in insect biology.

http://video.nationalgeographic.co.uk/video/player/kids/
animals-pets-kids/bugs-kids
The National Geographic video channel has some cool video clips about bug
superpowers, including some of the species mentioned in this book – dung
beetles, fires ants and jumping spiders.

PLACES TO GO

The Natural History Museum
Cromwell Road, London SW7 5BD
http://www.nhm.ac.uk

National Museum Cardiff
Cathays Park, Cardiff, CF10 3NP
http://www.museumwales.ac.uk/en/home/

National Museum of Scotland
Chambers Street, Edinburgh, EH1 1JF
http://www.nms.ac.uk

INDEX

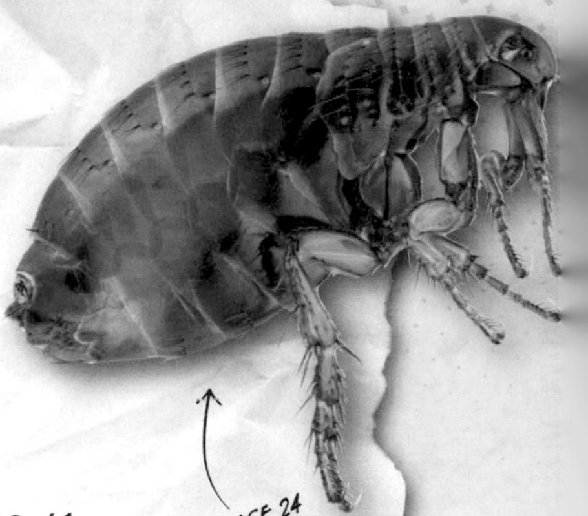

FLEA, PAGE 24

WIDOW SPIDER, PAGE 10

CONTENTS

Cinderella

I guess you think you know this story.
  You don't. The real one's much more gory.
The phoney one, the one you know,
Was cooked up years and years ago,
And made to sound all soft and sappy
Just to keep the children happy.
Mind you, they got the first bit right,
The bit where, in the dead of night,
The Ugly Sisters, jewels and all,
Departed for the Palace Ball,
While darling little Cinderella
Was locked up in a slimy cellar,
Where rats who wanted things to eat,
Began to nibble at her feet.

She bellowed 'Help!' and 'Let me out!'
The Magic Fairy heard her shout.
Appearing in a blaze of light,
She said, 'My dear, are you all right?'
'*All right?*' cried Cindy. 'Can't you see
'I feel as rotten as can be!'
She beat her fist against the wall,
And shouted, 'Get me to the Ball!
'There is a Disco at the Palace!
'The rest have gone and I am jalous!
'I want a dress! I want a coach!
'And earrings and a diamond brooch!
'And silver slippers, two of those!
'And lovely nylon panty-hose!
'Done up like that I'll guarantee
'The handsome Prince will fall for me!'
The Fairy said, 'Hang on a tick.'
She gave her wand a mighty flick
And quickly, in no time at all,
Cindy was at the Palace Ball!
It made the Ugly Sisters wince
To see her dancing with the Prince.
She held him very tight and pressed
Herself against his manly chest.
The Prince himself was turned to pulp,
All *he* could do was gasp and gulp.

Then midnight struck. She shouted, 'Heck!
'I've got to run to save my neck!'
The Prince cried, 'No! Alas! Alack!'
He grabbed her dress to hold her back.
As Cindy shouted, 'Let me go!'
The dress was ripped from head to toe.
She ran out in her underwear,
And lost one slipper on the stair.
The Prince was on it like a dart,
He pressed it to his pounding heart,
'The girl this slipper fits,' he cried,
'Tomorrow morn shall be my bride!
'I'll visit every house in town
'Until I've tracked the maiden down!'
Then rather carelessly, I fear,
He placed it on a crate of beer.
At once, one of the Ugly Sisters,
(The one whose face was blotched with blisters)
Sneaked up and grabbed the dainty shoe,
And quickly flushed it down the loo.

Then in its place she calmly put
The slipper from her own left foot.
Ah-ha, you see, the plot grows thicker,
And Cindy's luck starts looking sicker.
Next day, the Prince went charging down
To knock on all the doors in town.
In every house, the tension grew.
Who was the owner of the shoe?
The shoe was long and very wide.
(A normal foot got lost inside.)
Also it smelled a wee bit icky.
(The owner's feet were hot and sticky.)
Thousands of eager people came
To try it on, but all in vain.
Now came the Ugly Sisters' go.
One tried it on. The Prince screamed, 'No!'
But she screamed, 'Yes! It fits! Whoopee!
'So now you've got to marry me!'
The Prince went white from ear to ear.
He muttered, 'Let me out of here.'
'Oh no you don't! You made a vow!

'There's no way you can back out now!'
'Off with her head!' the Prince roared back.
They chopped it off with one big whack.
This pleased the Prince. He smiled and said,
'She's prettier without her head.'
Then up came Sister Number Two,
Who yelled, 'Now *I* will try the shoe!'
'Try this instead!' the Prince yelled back.
He swung his trusty sword and *smack* –
Her head went crashing to the ground.
It bounced a bit and rolled around.
In the kitchen, peeling spuds,
Cinderella heard the thuds
Of bouncing heads upon the floor,
And poked her own head round the door.
'What's all the racket?' Cindy cried.
'Mind your own bizz,' the Prince replied.
Poor Cindy's heart was torn to shreds.
My Prince! She thought. He chops off *heads*!

How could I marry anyone
Who does that sort of thing for fun?
The Prince cried, 'Who's this dirty slut?
'Off with her nut! Off with her nut!'
Just then, all in a blaze of light,
The Magic Fairy hove in sight,
Her Magic Wand went *swoosh* and *swish*!
'Cindy!' she cried, 'come make a wish!
'Wish anything and have no doubt
'That I will make it come about!'
Cindy answered, 'Oh kind Fairy,
'This time I shall be more wary.
'No more Princes, no more money.
'I have had my taste of honey.
'I'm wishing for a decent man.
'They're hard to find. D'you think you can?'
Within a minute, Cinderella
Was married to a lovely feller,
A simple jam-maker by trade,
Who sold good home-made marmalade.
Their house was filled with smiles and laughter
And they were happy ever after.

Jack and the Beanstalk

Jack's mother said, 'We're *stony broke*!
'Go out and find some wealthy bloke
'Who'll buy our cow. Just say she's sound
'And worth at least a hundred pound.
'But don't you dare to let him know
'That she's as old as billy-o.'
Jack led the old brown cow away,
And came back later in the day,
And said, 'Oh mumsie dear, guess what
'Your clever little boy has got.
'I got, I really don't know how,
'A super trade-in for our cow.'
The mother said, 'You little creep,
'I'll bet you sold her much too cheap.'

When Jack produced one lousy bean,
His startled mother, turning green,
Leaped high up in the air and cried,
'I'm *absolutely stupefied*!
'You crazy boy! D'you really mean
'You sold our Daisy for a bean?'
She snatched the bean. She yelled, 'You chump!'
And flung it on the rubbish-dump.
Then summoning up all her power,
She beat the boy for half an hour,
Using (and nothing could be meaner)
The handle of a vacuum-cleaner.
At ten p.m. or thereabout,
The little bean began to sprout.
By morning it had grown so tall
You couldn't see the top at all.
Young Jack cried, 'Mum, admit it now!
'It's better than a rotten cow!'
The mother said, 'You lunatic!
'Where are the beans that I can pick?
'There's not *one bean*! It's bare as bare!'
'No no!' cried Jack. 'You look up there!
'Look very high and you'll behold
'Each single leaf is solid gold!'
By gollikins, the boy was right!
Now, glistening in the morning light,
The mother actually perceives
A mass of lovely golden leaves!

She yells out loud, 'My sainted souls!
'I'll sell the Mini, buy a Rolls!
'Don't stand and gape, you little clot!
'Get up there quick and grab the lot!'
Jack was nimble, Jack was keen.
He scrambled up the mighty bean.
Up up he went without a stop,
But just as he was near the top,
A ghastly frightening thing occurred –
Not far above his head he heard
A big deep voice, a rumbling thing
That made the very heavens ring.
It shouted loud, 'FEE FI FO FUM
'I SMELL THE BLOOD OF AN
    ENGLISHMAN!'
Jack was frightened, Jack was quick,
And down he climbed in half a tick.

'Oh mum!' he gasped. 'Believe you me

'There's something nasty up our tree!

'I saw him, mum! My gizzard froze!

'A Giant with a clever nose!'

'*A clever nose*!' his mother hissed.

'You must be going round the twist!'

'He smelled me out, I swear it, mum!

'He said he *smelled* an Englishman!'

The mother said, 'And well he might!

'I've told you every single night

'To take a bath because you smell,

'But would you do it? Would you hell!

'You even make your mother shrink

'Because of your unholy stink!'

Jack answered, 'Well, if you're so clean

'Why don't *you* climb the crazy bean.'

The mother cried, 'By gad, I will!
'There's life within the old dog still!'
She hitched her skirts above her knee
And disappeared right up the tree.
Now would the Giant smell his mum?
Jack listened for the *fee-fo-fum*.
He gazed aloft. He wondered when
The dreaded words would come . . . And then . . .
From somewhere high above the ground
There came a frightful crunching sound.
He heard the Giant mutter twice,
'By gosh, that tasted very nice.
'Although' (and this in grumpy tones)
'I wish there weren't so many bones.'
'By Christopher!' Jack cried. 'By gum!
'The Giant's eaten up my mum!
'He smelled her out! She's in his belly!
'I had a hunch that she was smelly.'
Jack stood there gazing longingly
Upon the huge and golden tree.
He murmured softly, 'Golly-gosh,
'I guess I'll *have* to take a wash
'If I am going to climb this tree
'Without the Giant smelling me.
'In fact, a bath's my only hope . . .'
He rushed indoors and grabbed the soap.
He scrubbed his body everywhere.
He even washed and rinsed his hair.

He did his teeth, he blew his nose
And went out smelling like a rose.
Once more he climbed the mighty bean.
The Giant sat there, gross, obscene,
Muttering through his vicious teeth
(While Jack sat tensely just beneath),
Muttering loud, 'FEE FI FO FUM,
'RIGHT NOW I CAN'T SMELL ANYONE.'
Jack waited till the Giant slept,
Then out along the boughs he crept
And gathered so much gold, I swear
He was an instant millionaire.
'A bath,' he said, 'does seem to pay.
'I'm going to have one every day.'

Snow-White and the Seven Dwarfs

When little Snow-White's mother died,
The king, her father, up and cried,
'Oh, what a nuisance! What a life!
'Now I must find another wife!'
(It's never easy for a king
To find himself that sort of thing.)
He wrote to every magazine
And said, 'I'm looking for a Queen.'
At least ten thousand girls replied
And begged to be the royal bride.
The king said with a shifty smile,
'I'd like to give each one a trial.'
However, in the end he chose
A lady called Miss Maclahose,
Who brought along a curious toy
That seemed to give her endless joy –
This was a mirror framed in brass,
A MAGIC TALKING LOOKING-GLASS.
Ask it something day or night,
It always got the answer right.
For instance, if you were to say,
'Oh Mirror, what's for lunch today?'
The thing would answer in a trice,

'Today it's scrambled eggs and rice.'
Now every day, week in week out,
The spoiled and stupid Queen would shout,
'Oh Mirror Mirror on the wall,
'Who is the fairest of them all?'
The Mirror answered every time,
'Oh Madam, you're the Queen sublime.
'You are the only one to charm us,
'Queen, you are the cat's pyjamas.'
For ten whole years the silly Queen
Repeated this absurd routine.
Then suddenly, one awful day,
She heard the Magic Mirror say,
'From now on, Queen, you're *Number Two.*
'*Snow-White* is prettier than you!'
The Queen went absolutely wild.
She yelled, 'I'm going to scrag that child!

'I'll cook her flaming goose! I'll skin'er!
'I'll have her rotten guts for dinner!'
She called the Huntsman to her study.
She shouted at him, 'Listen, buddy!
'You drag that filthy girl outside,
'And see you take her for a ride!
'Thereafter slit her ribs apart
'And bring me back her bleeding heart!'
The Huntsman dragged the lovely child
Deep deep into the forest wild.

Fearing the worst, poor Snow-White spake.
She cried, 'Oh please give me a break!'
The knife was poised, the arm was strong,
She cried again, 'I've done no *wrong*!'
The Huntsman's heart began to flutter.
It melted like a pound of butter.
He murmured, 'Okay, beat it, kid,'
And you can bet your life she did.

Later, the Huntsman made a stop
Within the local butcher's shop,
And there he bought, for safety's sake,
A bullock's heart and one nice steak.

'Oh Majesty! Oh Queen!' he cried,
'That rotten little girl has died!
'And just to prove I didn't cheat,
'I've brought along these bits of meat.'
The Queen cried out, 'Bravissimo!
'I trust you killed her nice and slow.'
Then (this is the disgusting part)
The Queen sat down and ate the heart!
(I only hope she cooked it well.
Boiled heart can be as tough as hell.)
While all of this was going on,
Oh where, oh where had Snow-White gone?
She'd found it easy, being pretty,
To hitch a ride into the city,
And there she'd got a job, unpaid,
As general cook and parlour-maid
With seven funny little men,
Each one not more than three foot ten,
Ex horse-race jockeys, all of them.

These Seven Dwarfs, though awfully nice,
Were guilty of one shocking vice –
They squandered all of their resources
At the race-track backing horses.
(When they hadn't backed a winner,
None of them got any dinner.)
One evening, Snow-White said, 'Look here,
'I think I've got a great idea.
'Just leave it all to me, okay?
'And no more gambling till I say.'
That very night, at eventide,
Young Snow-White hitched another ride,
And then, when it was very late,
She slipped in through the Palace gate.
The King was in his counting house
Counting out his money,
The Queen was in the parlour
Eating bread and honey,
The footmen and the servants slept
So no one saw her as she crept
On tip-toe through the mighty hall
And grabbed THE MIRROR off the wall.
As soon as she had got it home,
She told the Senior Dwarf (or Gnome)
To ask it what he wished to know.
'Go on!' she shouted. 'Have a go!'
He said, 'Oh Mirror, please don't joke!
'Each one of us is stony broke!
'Which horse will win tomorrow's race,

'The Ascot Gold Cup Steeplechase?'
The Mirror whispered sweet and low,
'The horse's name is Mistletoe.'
The Dwarfs went absolutely daft,
They kissed young Snow-White fore and aft,
Then rushed away to raise some dough
With which to back old Mistletoe.
They pawned their watches, sold the car,
They borrowed money near and far,
(For much of it they had to thank
The manager of Barclays Bank.)
They went to Ascot and of course
For once they backed the winning horse.
Thereafter, every single day,
The Mirror made the bookies pay.
Each Dwarf and Snow-White got a share,
And each was soon a millionaire,
Which shows that gambling's not a sin
Provided that you always win.

Goldilocks and the Three Bears

This famous wicked little tale
Should never have been put on sale.
It is a mystery to me
Why loving parents cannot see
That this is actually a book
About a brazen little crook.
Had I the chance I wouldn't fail
To clap young Goldilocks in jail.
Now just imagine how *you'd* feel
If you had cooked a lovely meal,
Delicious porridge, steaming hot,
Fresh coffee in the coffee-pot,
With maybe toast and marmalade,
The table beautifully laid,
One place for you and one for dad,
Another for your little lad.
Then dad cries, 'Golly-gosh! Gee-whizz!
'Oh cripes! How hot this porridge is!

'Let's take a walk along the street
'Until it's cool enough to eat.'
He adds, 'An early morning stroll
'Is good for people on the whole.
'It makes your appetite improve
'It also helps your bowels to move.'
No proper wife would dare to question
Such a sensible suggestion,
Above all not at breakfast-time
When men are seldom at their prime.
No sooner are you down the road
Than Goldilocks, that little toad,
That nosey thieving little louse,
Comes sneaking in your empty house.
She looks around. She quickly notes
Three bowls brimful of porridge oats.
And while still standing on her feet,
She grabs a spoon and starts to eat.

I say again, how *would* you feel
If you had made this lovely meal
And some delinquent little tot
Broke in and gobbled up the lot?

But wait! That's not the worst of it!
Now comes the most distressing bit.
You are of course a houseproud wife,
And all your happy married life
You have collected lovely things
Like gilded cherubs wearing wings,
And furniture by Chippendale
Bought at some famous auction sale.
But your most special valued treasure,
The piece that gives you endless pleasure,
Is one small children's dining-chair,
Elizabethan, very rare.
It is in fact your joy and pride,
Passed down to you on grandma's side.
But Goldilocks, like many freaks,
Does not appreciate antiques.
She doesn't care, she doesn't mind,
And now she plonks her fat behind
Upon this dainty precious chair,
And crunch! It busts beyond repair.
A nice girl would at once exclaim,
'Oh dear! Oh heavens! What a shame!'

Not Goldie. She begins to swear.
She bellows, 'What a lousy chair!'
And uses *one* disgusting word
That luckily you've never heard.
(I dare not write it, even hint it.
Nobody would ever print it.)
You'd think by now this little skunk
Would have the sense to do a bunk.
But no. I very much regret
She hasn't nearly finished yet.
Deciding she would like a rest,
She says, 'Let's see which bed is best.'
Upstairs she goes and tries all three.
(Here comes the next catastrophe.)
Most educated people choose
To rid themselves of socks and shoes
Before they clamber into bed.
But Goldie didn't give a shred.
Her filthy shoes were thick with grime,
And mud and mush and slush and slime.
Worse still, upon the heel of one
Was something that a dog had done.
I say once more, what *would* you think
If all this horrid dirt and stink
Was smeared upon your eiderdown
By this revolting little clown?
(The famous story has no clues
To show the girl removed her shoes.)

Oh, what a tale of crime on crime!
Let's check it for a second time.

Crime One, the prosecution's case:
She breaks and enters someone's place.

Crime Two, the prosecutor notes:
She steals a bowl of porridge oats.

Crime Three: She breaks a precious chair
Belonging to the Baby Bear.

Crime Four: She smears each spotless sheet
With filthy messes from her feet.

A judge would say without a blink,
'Ten years hard labour in the clink!'
But in the book, as you will see,
The little beast gets off scot-free,
While tiny children near and far
Shout, 'Goody-good! Hooray! Hurrah!'
'Poor darling Goldilocks!' they say,
'Thank goodness that she got away!'
Myself, I think I'd rather send
Young Goldie to a sticky end.
'Oh daddy!' cried the Baby Bear,
'My porridge gone! It isn't fair!'
'Then go upstairs,' the Big Bear said,
'Your porridge is upon the bed.
'But as it's inside mademoiselle,
'You'll have to eat *her* up as well.'

Little Red Riding Hood and the Wolf

As soon as Wolf began to feel
That he would like a decent meal,
He went and knocked on Grandma's door.
When Grandma opened it, she saw
The sharp white teeth, the horrid grin,
And Wolfie said, 'May I come in?'
Poor Grandmamma was terrified,
'He's going to eat me up,' she cried.
And she was absolutely right.
He ate her up in one big bite.
But Grandmamma was small and tough,
And Wolfie wailed, 'That's not enough!
'I haven't yet begun to feel
'That I have had a decent meal!'
He ran around the kitchen yelping,
'I've *got* to have another helping!'
Then added with a frightful leer,
'I'm therefore going to wait right here
'Till Little Miss Red Riding Hood
'Comes home from walking in the wood.'
He quickly put on Grandma's clothes.
(Of course he hadn't eaten those.)

He dressed himself in coat and hat.
He put on shoes and after that
He even brushed and curled his hair,
Then sat himself in Grandma's chair.
In came the little girl in red.
She stopped. She stared. And then she said,

'*What great big ears you have, Grandma.*'
'*All the better to hear you with,*' the Wolf replied.
'*What great big eyes you have, Grandma,*'
     said Little Red Riding Hood.
'*All the better to see you with,*' the Wolf replied.

He sat there watching her and smiled.
He thought, I'm going to eat this child.
Compared with her old Grandmamma
She's going to taste like caviare.

Then Little Red Riding Hood said, '*But Grandma,
what a lovely great big furry coat you have on.*'

'That's wrong!' cried Wolf. 'Have you forgot
'To tell me what BIG TEETH I've got?
'Ah well, no matter what you say,
'I'm going to eat you anyway.'
The small girl smiles. One eyelid flickers.
She whips a pistol from her knickers.
She aims it at the creature's head
And *bang bang bang,* she shoots him dead.
A few weeks later, in the wood,
I came across Miss Riding Hood.
But what a change! No cloak of red,
No silly hood upon her head.
She said, 'Hello, and do please note
'My lovely furry WOLFSKIN COAT.'

The Three Little Pigs

The animal I really dig
  Above all others is the pig.
Pigs are noble. Pigs are clever,
Pigs are courteous. However,
Now and then, to break this rule,
One meets a pig who is a fool.
What, for example, would you say
If strolling through the woods one day,
Right there in front of you you saw
A pig who'd built his house of STRAW?
The Wolf who saw it licked his lips,
And said, 'That pig has had his chips.'

'Little pig, little pig, let me come in!'
'No, no, by the hairs on my chinny-chin-chin!'
'Then I'll huff and I'll puff and I'll blow your
house in!'

The little pig began to pray,
But Wolfie blew his house away.
He shouted, 'Bacon, pork and ham!
'Oh, what a lucky Wolf I am!'
And though he ate the pig quite fast,
He carefully kept the tail till last.
Wolf wandered on, a trifle bloated.
Surprise, surprise, for soon he noted
Another little house for pigs,
And this one had been built of TWIGS!

'Little pig, little pig, let me come in!'
'No, no, by the hairs of my chinny-chin-chin!'
'Then I'll huff and I'll puff and I'll blow your
house in!'

The Wolf said 'Okay, here we go!'
He then began to blow and blow.
The little pig began to squeal.
He cried, 'Oh Wolf, you've had *one* meal!
'Why can't we talk and make a deal?'
The Wolf replied, 'Not on your nelly!'
And soon the pig was in his belly.
'Two juicy little pigs!' Wolf cried,
'But still I am not satisfied!
'I know full well my tummy's bulging,
'But oh, how I adore indulging.'

So creeping quietly as a mouse,
The Wolf approached another house,
A house which also had inside
A little piggy trying to hide.
But this one, Piggy Number Three,
Was bright and brainy as could be.
No straw for him, no twigs or sticks.
This pig had built his house of BRICKS.
'You'll not get *me*!' the Piggy cried.
'I'll blow you down!' the Wolf replied.
'You'll need,' Pig said, 'a lot of puff,
'And I don't think you've got enough.'
Wolf huffed and puffed and blew and blew.
The house stayed up as good as new.
'If I can't blow it *down*,' Wolf said,
'I'll have to blow it *up* instead.
'I'll come back in the dead of night
'And blow it up with dynamite!'
Pig cried, 'You brute! I might have known!'
Then, picking up the telephone,
He dialled as quickly as he could
The number of Red Riding Hood.

'Hello,' she said. 'Who's speaking? *Who?*
'Oh, hello Piggy, how d'you do?'
Pig cried, 'I need your help, Miss Hood!
'Oh help me, please! D'you think you could?'
'I'll try, of course,' Miss Hood replied.
'What's on your mind?' . . . '*A Wolf!*' Pig cried.
'I know you've dealt with wolves before,
'And now I've got one at my door!'
'My darling Pig,' she said, 'my sweet,
'That's something *really* up my street.
'I've just begun to wash my hair.
'But when it's dry, I'll be right there.'
A short while later, through the wood,
Came striding brave Miss Riding Hood.
The Wolf stood there, his eyes ablaze
And yellowish, like mayonnaise.
His teeth were sharp, his gums were raw,
And spit was dripping from his jaw.

Once more the maiden's eyelid flickers.
She draws the pistol from her knickers.
Once more, she hits the vital spot,
And kills him with a single shot.
Pig, peeping through the window, stood
And yelled, 'Well done, Miss Riding Hood!'

Ah, Piglet, you must never trust
Young ladies from the upper crust.
For now, Miss Riding Hood, one notes,
Not only has *two* wolfskin coats,
But when she goes from place to place,
She has a PIGSKIN TRAVELLING CASE.

Contents

What is pushing?

Pushing is one way to move something away from you.

You can push a **buggy** to move it.

Some things are easy to push.

Other things are hard to push.

How hard do you have to push?

The **climbing frame** is heavy.

You need to push it into the corner.

Push the climbing frame.

You have to push hard to move it over the **rough** carpet.

Now the **climbing frame** is on the **smooth** floor.

Will you have to push hard now?

You only have to push a little.

It is easier to push on a smooth floor.

Can you push something heavier than you?

You dropped some of your crayons under the chair.

Can you move the chair to get them?

Try to push the chair.

It is too heavy for you.

Ask a friend to help you.

Together you can push the chair.

More people means more
pushing power.

Now you can colour with all
your crayons!

Which handle is for pushing?

There are pieces of paper on the floor.

You need to tidy up.

You can push the paper with
a brush.

What kind of **handle** can you use?

A rope **handle** will not work.

The rope will not stay **stiff**.

A wooden handle will stay stiff.

You need a stiff handle
for pushing.

Can you push down to push something up?

This is a **pogo stick**.

You can balance on it.

If you stand on the footrests you push the pogo stick down.

What happens when you push down on the **pogo stick**?

You will bounce up.

The harder you push down, the higher you bounce.

Quiz

Will it be harder to push the truck through the **rough** sand or across the **smooth** floor?

Look for the answer on page 24.

Glossary

buggy
pushchair for babies and young children

climbing frame
framework that you climb on for fun and exercise

handle
part used to pick up, open or hold something

pogo stick
toy for bouncing on

rough
uneven or bumpy surface

smooth
even surface that is not bumpy or rough

stiff
not easy to bend or change in shape

Index

Answer to quiz on page 22

It is harder to push the toy through the rough sand.

 CAUTION: Children should not attempt any experiment without an adult's help and permission.

24